NEW DIMENSIONS *in*
AFRICAN HISTORY

NEW DIMENSIONS *in* AFRICAN HISTORY

The London Lectures of
Dr. Yosef ben-Jochannan
and **Dr. John Henrik Clarke**

Edited with Introduction by
Dr. John Henrik Clarke

Africa World Press, Inc.

P.O. Box 1892
Trenton, New Jersey 08607

Africa World Press, Inc.

P.O. Box 1892
Trenton, New Jersey 08607

Book design and typesetting by Malcolm Litchfield
This book is composed in ITC Galliard

Library of Congress Catalog Card Number: 91-70616

ISBN: 0-86543-226-0   Cloth
          0-86543-227-9   Paper

Contents

Explanatory Note   vii

Introduction   1

The Real Story of the Scramble for Africa   15
  Dr. Yosef ben-Jochannan

African Resistance and Colonial Domination: The Africans
  in the Americas   24
  Dr. John Henrik Clarke

  Questions and Answers   35

The African Contribution to Technology and Science   55
  Dr. Yosef ben-Jochannan

The Africans in the New World: Their Contribution to
  Science, Invention and Technology   63
  Dr. John Henrik Clarke

  Questions and Answers   72

v

The Nile Valley Civilization and the Spread of African
    Culture   83
      Dr. Yosef ben-Jochannan

Pan-Africanism and the Future of the African Family   97
      Dr. John Henrik Clarke

  Questions and Answers   108

An Interview with Yosef ben-Jochannan   129
      Carole A. Parks

A Search for Identity   131
      Dr. John Henrik Clarke

Reading Guide for the Study and Teaching of African
    World History   141

  1 Africa's Place in World History from the
    Origin of Man to 1600 A.D.   145
  2 Africa's Place in World History from 1600 A.D.
    to the Present   166
  3 Africa's Place in African-American History
    from Slavery to Emancipation   180
  4 Africa's Place in African-American History
    from the Reconstruction to the Present   193

Bibliography   205

EXPLANATORY NOTE

These lectures were delivered for the Minority Ethnic Unit of the Greater London Council, London, England, March 6-8, 1986. They were addressed mainly to the African community in London consisting of African people from the Caribbean and African people from Africa.

These lectures are being published here with additional material because both Dr. Yosef ben-Jochannan and I are veterans in the field of teaching African world history and we have had a number of requests for these lectures in book form.

Dr. John Henrik Clarke

Dedicated

to

Gertrude Johannes Jochannan for her years of devotion as wife
and mother and for understanding the nature of our mission—the
total restoration of African world history

and

Sybil C. Williams for her commitment to African world liberation
and for the encouragement and warmth we have found in her
friendship.

INTRODUCTION

I n order to create an excuse and a rationale for the slave trade
and the colonial system that followed it, Europeans had to
forget, or pretend to forget, all they had previously known
about Africa, African history, African people and their culture. In
one of his last public speeches on this subject the Caribbean writer,
historian and political activist, the late Richard B. Moore observed:

> The significance of African history is shown, though not
> overtly, in the very effort to deny anything worthy of the name
> of history to Africa and the African peoples. This widespread,
> and well nigh successful endeavor, maintained through some
> five centuries, to erase African history from the general record,
> is a fact which of itself should be quite conclusive to thinking
> and open minds. For it is logical and apparent that no such
> undertaking would ever have been carried on, and at such
> length, in order to obscure and bury what is actually of little
> or no significance.
>
> The prime significance of African history becomes still more
> manifest when it is realized that this deliberate denial of
> African history arose out of the European expansion and
> invasion of Africa which began in the middle of the fifteenth
> century. The compulsion was thereby felt to attempt to justify
> such colonialist conquest, domination, enslavement and plun-
> der. Hence, this brash denial of history and culture to Africa,

1

and indeed even of human qualities and capacity for "civilization" to the indigenous peoples of Africa.

Mr. Moore is saying, in essence, that African history must be looked at anew and seen in its relationship to world history. First, the distortions must be admitted. The hard fact is that most of what we now call world history is only the history of the first and second rise of Europe. The Europeans are not yet willing to acknowledge that the world did not wait in darkness for them to bring the light. The history of Africa was already old when Europe was born.

Until quite recently, it was rather generally assumed, even among well educated persons in the West, that the continent of Africa was a great expanse of land, mostly jungle, inhabited by savages and fierce beasts. It was not thought of as an area where great civilizations could have existed or where the great kings of these civilizations could have ruled in might and wisdom over vast empires. It is true that there were some notions current about the cultural achievements of Egypt, but Egypt was conceived of as European land rather than as a country of Africa. Even if a look at an atlas or globe showed Egypt to be in Africa, the popular thought immediately saw in the Sahara a formidable barrier and a convenient division of Africa into two parts: one (north of the Sahara) was inhabited by European-like people of high culture and noble history; the other (south of the Sahara) was inhabited by dark-skinned people who had no culture, and were incapable of having done anything in their dark and distant past that could be dignified by the designation of "history." Such ideas, of course, are far from the truth, as we shall see. But it is not difficult to understand why they persisted, and unfortunately still persist, in one form or another in the popular mind.

Our own great historian, W. E. B. DuBois, tells us:

Always Africa is giving us something new.... On its black bosom arose one of the earliest, if not the earliest, of self-protecting civilizations, and grew so mightily that it still furnishes superlatives to thinking and speaking men. Out of its darker and more remote forest fastnesses came, if we may credit many recent scientists, the first welding of iron, and we know that agriculture and trade flourished there when Europe was a wilderness.

It is too often forgotten that more than five thousand years had unfolded before what was to become Europe was a political factor in world affairs.

When the early Europeans first met Africans, at the crossroads of history, it was a respectful meeting and the Africans were not slaves. Their nations were old before Europe was born. In this period of history, what was to be later known as "Africa" was an unknown place to the people who would someday be called "Europeans." Only the people of some of the Mediterranean islands and a few states of what would become the Greek and Roman states knew of part of North Africa, and that was a land of mystery. After the rise and decline of Greek civilization and the Roman destruction of the city of Carthage, they made one area of the conquered territories into a province which they called Africa, a word derived from "afri" and the name of a group of people about whom little is known. At first the word applied only to the Roman colonies of North Africa. There was a time when all dark-skinned people were called "Ethiopians," for the Greeks referred to Africa as "the Land of the Burnt-face People."

If Africa, in general, is a man-made mystery, Egypt, in particular, is a bigger one. There has long been an attempt on the part of some European "scholars" to deny that Egypt was a part of Africa. To do this they had to ignore the great masterpieces on Egyptian history written by European writers such as *Ancient Egypt, Light of the World, Vols. I and II*, and a whole school of European thought that placed Egypt in proper focus in relationship to the rest of Africa.

The distorters of African history also had to ignore the fact that the people of the ancient land which would later be called Egypt never called their country by that name. It was called *Ta-Merry* or *Kampt* and sometimes *Kemet* or *Sais*. The ancient Hebrews called it Mizrain. Later the Moslem Arabs used the same term but later discarded it. Both the Greeks and the Romans referred to the country as "the Pearl of the Nile." The Greeks gave it the simple name *Aegyptcus*. Thus the word we know as Egypt is of Greek origin.

Until recent times most Western scholars have been reluctant to call attention to the fact that the Nile River is 4,000 miles long. It starts in the south, in the heart of Africa, and flows to the north. It was the world's first cultural highway making Egypt a composite of many African cultures. In his article "The Lost Pharaohs of Nubia," Professor Bruce Williams infers that the nations in the south could be older than Egypt. This information is not new. When rebel European scholars were saying this one hundred years ago, and proving it, they were not taken seriously.

It is unfortunate that so much of the history of Africa has been written by conquerors, foreigners, missionaries and adventurers. The Egyptians left the best record of their history, written by local writers. It was not until near the end of the eighteenth century when a few European scholars learned to decipher their writing that this was understood.

The Greek traveler, Herodotus, was in Africa in about 450 B.C. His eyewitness account is still a revelation. He witnessed African civilization in decline and partly in ruins, after many invasions. However, he could still see the indications of the greatness that it had been. In this period in history, the Nile Valley civilization of Africa had already brought forth two "Golden Ages" of achievement and had left its mark for all the world to see.

In his book, *African Origin of Civilization: Myth or Reality*, the African historian Cheikh Anta Diop has said, in effect, that the history of Africa will be out of kilter until Egypt is seen in proper focus in relationship to the rest of Africa. Professor Chancellor Williams calls the second chapter of his book, *The Destruction of Black Civilization*, "Ethiopia's Oldest Daughter: Egypt." In this chapter Professor Williams writes a short history of the people that the Greeks later called "Egyptians." He explains the circumstances of their migration from the Upper to the Lower Nile River. In two different books, *Abu-Simbel—Ghizeh, Guide Book/Manual* and *Black Man of the Nile and His Family*, Professor ben-Jochannan has presented new evidence on the southern African origins of Egypt from their own writings. In his statement he says:

This guide book, or manual, will concentrate on those many aspects which depicted the indigenous African contributions to the high-culture of Ta-Merry-Nubia that reached its first zenith before the original foreign invaders of Africa, called "Hyksos" or "Shepherd Kings of Bedunia," in ca. 1675 B.C.E., XIIIth Dynasty, conquered the Delta Region of Egypt, Northeast Africa.

My reason for emphasizing the indigenous Southern African origin of the ancient Egyptians, who were equally, "Africans," is based upon an historical message extracted from the highly respected "Papyrus of Hunefer" found in the Egyptians' and other Nile Valley indigenous Africans' *Book of the Coming Forth by Day and Night;* thus:

We came from the beginning of the Nile where the God Hapi dwells, at the foothills of the mountain of the moon. (Kilimanjaro—between Kenya and Tanzania, or Rwenzori in Uganda).

There is no attempt there at settling the issue of the "racial" and or "indigenous physical characteristics" of the ancient Egyptians or Nubians. I will concentrate on the type, quality and reason for the colossal monuments, artifacts, and other remaining effects of the Lower Nile with respect to Egypt— "The Gift of the Nile" as Nubia.

The breakdown of the "Pre-Dynastic" and the "Dynastic," along with the "Post-Dynastic."

This was the first age of grandeur for the Nile Valley High Culture. It lasted until the eve of the Christian era. Some aspects of it survived the Greek and Roman occupation of parts of North Africa. After 300 A.D., new states and eventually empires began to appear in Inner West Africa that the Arabs later called the Western Sudan. The best known of these states are Ghana, Mali and Songhay. Their collective life span was more than a thousand years. Some of these independent states in West Africa were in the process of decline on the eve of the slave trade.

The Atlantic slave trade and the rationale used to justify it locked African history into what Professor Ivan Van Sertima has called "the five hundred year room." For five hundred years the history of African people has been, mainly, interpreted by non-Africans who did not have their interest at heart. The story of Africa before the trans-Atlantic slave trade is generally unknown. Slavery is only one factor in African history and that too is misunderstood. For most of the years African people have been in the world, they have been a free, self-governing people.

Africans were great makers of culture long before their first appearance in Jamestown, Virginia, in 1619. The rich and colorful history, art and folklore in West Africa, the ancestral home of most African-Americans, presents evidence of this, and more.

Contrary to a misconception which still prevails, the Africans were familiar with literature and art for many years before their contact with the Western world. Before the breaking up of the social structure of the West African states of Ghana, Mali and Songhay, and the internal strife and chaos that made the slave trade possible, the forefathers of the Africans who eventually became slaves in the United States lived in a society where university life was fairly common and scholars were beheld with reverence.

There were in this ancestry rulers who expanded their kingdoms into empires, great and magnificent armies whose physical dimensions dwarfed entire nations into submission, generals who advanced the technique of military science, scholars whose vision of life showed foresight and wisdom and priests who told of gods that were strong and kind. To understand fully any aspect of African-American life, one must realize that the Black American is not without a cultural past, though he was many generations removed from it before his achievement in American literature and art commanded any appreciable attention.

I have been referring to the African origin of African-American literature and history. This preface is essential to every meaningful discussion of the role of the African-American in every major aspect of American life, past and present.

Africans Away from Home

The Africans who were brought against their will across the Atlantic never fully adjusted to slavery or accepted it as something that was inevitable. Instead, they pursued liberty under trying and seemingly impossible conditions, and their search continued throughout the entire period of their enslavement.

The real fight for liberty by these Africans started on the shores of Africa and in the slave-holding forts along the West African coast. As many slaves were forced onto the slave ships they picked up a handful of African dirt and forced it into their mouths in their determination to take some of their homeland with them as they went into forced exile.

This pursuit of liberty and lost nationhood continued in the form of revolts on the slave ships. During exercise periods, when Africans were brought up on the deck for air, many of them jumped overboard. The masters of the slave ships also discovered that some on board had merely committed suicide while some Africans were killed when they attempted to assault those who enslaved them on the ships.

This spirit of revolt was nurtured throughout slavery and took many forms wherever slaves were found, whether in South America, in the Caribbean, or in the United States.

South America and the Caribbean

In South America the slave revolts were most successful in Brazil and other areas where there were large areas of thick forest and wooded hills. Many Africans escaped the auction blocks and headed for the forests and hills where they were able to form separate African communities. These escaped Africans were later referred to as maroons.

The large number of Africans imported into Brazil came from diverse cultures in Africa, but, under the pressure of slavery, they managed to settle their cultural differences and work together for liberty. Scattered communities of these escaped Africans existed throughout the Americas, not only in the swamps and forests of Brazil but also in the hills of Haiti and Jamaica in the Caribbean.

Africans in Brazil established two separate states, Bahia and Palmares. The slaves in Bahia surrendered under military pressure from the Portuguese. However, Palmares existed for at least 110 years, until 1695. It remained a rough-hewn African republic until Portuguese and other Europeans living on the edge of Palmares helped the Portuguese government lead a superior military force to the area and destroyed the state. The heroic stand these Africans took in defense of their state is a proud page in the story of how Africans pursued liberty away from home.

In other parts of South America, in the countries now called Guyana and Surinam, there was an uprising in the area of Berbice that became known as the Berbice Revolt. These revolts in Guyana and in Surinam were referred to as the Bush Negro Rebellions. The important thing about the revolts mentioned here is that they occurred before the American Revolution. Therefore, these Africans in the Americas led the *first* revolts against tyranny in the New World.

The Caribbean Islands, like the plantations of South America, were incubators for revolts by slaves pursuing liberty in the New World. Because of the need for slave labor in the plantation system and the economic recovery of Europe after 1492, slavery was most harsh on islands that produced the largest economic benefits for Europeans. The first revolt of African slaves, where the record is clear, occurred in Cuba in 1527, but most of the organized revolts started on the islands of Haiti and Jamaica.

The greatest Caribbean revolts in pursuit of liberty occurred in Jamaica prior to the Haitian Revolution. The Jamaicans fought longer and harder than the Haitians, but they failed to gain their independence because the British had a small internal military force in Jamaica. There were also numerous mulattoes who had not decided where their loyalties lay. The mulattoes did not join in the African revolt because they assumed that they would be fighting against their own white fathers. The Africans in Haiti were able to gain their independence and establish a free state because France, which had many other military entanglements, did not have sufficient able troops to send to Haiti and put down a revolt.

The South American and Caribbean revolts in pursuit of liberty were successful partly for reasons of geography but more importantly because of African cultural continuity. This phenomenon is best understood by considering briefly the buying customs of the British slave masters in South America and the Caribbean. They generally bought slaves in large lots and kept the lots together. Therefore, many Africans who were captured in the same general areas of West

Africa maintained their African religion, language, and in a general sense, their cultural continuity. In the United States, however, slaves were generally bought in small lots and resold before the end of the week. Families and cultural continuity were broken to such an extent that often, after a month in the United States, many slaves could not even identify other slaves who arrived with them on the same boat.

The conditions of slavery were not less brutal in South America or in the Caribbean than they were in the United States, but greater cultural continuity was maintained. It was this factor that facilitated the slave revolts in the West Indies and in South America. Organized African resistance to conditions in these areas occurred with a greater consistency, due to the fact that the slaves who were house servants still had loyalty to the other slaves who were field workers.

The revolts by slaves in South America and the Caribbean started 100 years before 1619, when slaves formally arrived in the British colony that became known as the United States, and before the arrival of the Mayflower in 1620.

Early Years in the United States

In the United States, the African pursuit of liberty differed in various parts of the country, depending on conditions at the respective plantations, relationships forged with other ethnic groups, the impact of weather, and contacts with Africans from the Caribbean.

The African slaves who arrived in Jamestown, Virginia, in 1619 were not chattel slaves, in the general sense; they were indentured servants. Lerone Bennett has explained very graphically in the early chapters of his book, *The Shaping of Black America*, the conditions under which these early arrivals lived. He explains that most of the first indentured servants and those that arrived for the next 100 years were white. He also explains that Africans could have inherited their chains from the Indians and poor whites, both of whom were indentured servants in large numbers before the arrival of Africans.

White and Indian Allies

The years between 1619 and 1776 sometimes have been referred to as the lost or neglected years in the history of slavery in the United

States. During this period, many whites worked their way out of indenture, some joined the slave system, and still others opposed it. The idea of prejudice based solely on color had not crystallized in the minds of the poor whites, who had no vested interest in the maintenance of the slave system. White indentured servants and many other poor whites generally had no derogatory attitude towards the Africans. Some of them worked side-by-side on the same farms. There are also many recorded incidents where indentured whites joined Africans in revolt against the conditions of slavery and in their mutual pursuit of liberty.

Bennett further tells us that Africans in pursuit of liberty often escaped and lived among the indigenous Americans, known as Indians. The best known incident of this nature occurred in the Everglades of Florida.

At one period in history, over half the army of the Seminole Indians consisted of escaped African slaves. There were so many Africans in the ranks of the Indian army that one military officer fighting the Indians, observing that most of the Indian army were escaped slaves, remarked that this was no longer an "Indian" war.

This condition existed throughout the Seminole Wars. The heroic stands that Indians and slaves made together, as allies during the formative years of the United States and in what is referred to as the Seminole Wars, is still another chapter in the pursuit of liberty by Africans in America.

New England Weather

The pursuit of liberty differed in New England because of the weather. Many of the slaves there worked in industry and also worked as carpenters, plasterers, and ships' caulkers. The winters in New England are long, and therefore there was no need for Africans to labor all year round as slaves in these industries.

The value of the slave differed appreciably in the New England states from those on southern plantations. In New England, many slaves bought their liberty, some escaped into Canada through the underground railroad, and others were freed by Quakers who no longer believed in the slave system. As a result, a small contingent of African freedmen began to emerge in New England.

Caribbean Influences

Freedmen had already emerged in the Caribbean, mainly on the island of Jamaica. On the eve of the American Revolution these Africans began to make contact with Africans in North America, unifying their efforts in pursuit of liberty for all Africans away from home. This could have been the first inkling of the concept that would later be identified as Pan-Africanism.

This was also the period when Prince Hall, a former slave from Barbados, now a free man, came to the New England colony and joined forces with the Black American freedmen. He was told that if he owned property, he would get consideration, so he brought property. This did not appreciably change his condition or that of other Blacks. He was told that ministers got respect, so he became a minister, but this did not change his condition either.

Finally Prince Hall decided to start a fraternal organization. He requested a charter from the British but was turned down. A Scottish and Irish regiment which was serving under the British gave him an authentic charter for the organization now referred to as the Masons. They used this charter until the British reconsidered their request and sent them a charter three years later. This is recorded in a book, *Prince Hall: Life and Legacy* by Charles H. Wesley. Prince Hall then established the first Black Masonic order in the United States, calling his organization the African Lodge. He used this order to continue the African pursuit of liberty, calling attention to the condition of Africans still not free. In New England, the African Lodge served as the inspiration for the beginning of other independent Black organizations. Its success also led eventually to the establishment of an independent Black church, the African Methodist Episcopal Church, under the leadership of Richard Allen.

Continued collaboration between Caribbean freedmen and Black American freed men in New England created an atmosphere that encouraged slaves in the south to escape, knowing that there were people to protect them if they succeeded. This made it possible for Frederick Douglass, who had the will to escape from slavery, to develop his talents and emerge as a national leader.

Protests in Word and Deed

The pursuit of liberty by Africans in the United States took several different forms. It began with questions they asked about contradictions inherent in proclaiming a revolution, announcing liberty and justice for all, but not including Black Americans.

The radical Black ministry that began to emerge during the first half of the nineteenth century, filled with ideas about the American Revolution, saw these contradictions and set in motion several massive slave revolts. There was the Gabriel Prosser revolt in 1800, the Denmark Vesey revolt in 1822, and the best known of all, the Nat Turner revolt in Virginia that occurred in 1831.

Also during the first half of the nineteenth century a literature of protest and revolt had emerged in such Black-edited publications as *Freedom's Journal*, a newspaper operated by Frederick Douglass called *The North Star* and later *Douglass' Monthly*. Douglass was a most able leader and the most eloquent voice of the African people's pursuit of liberty. In 1829 David Walker issued his famous *Appeal to the Colored People of the World* summoning them to revolt against their condition. There were also great figures like Martin Delany, Henry Highland Garnett, Samuel Ringgold Ward and others who emerged in this period.

The continuous attacks by Black abolitionists on the eve of the Civil War focused on slavery and the conditions of slavery, and they created a great deal of antislavery sentiments. During the Civil War, Black Americans fought in large numbers on the side of the North, especially the famous Black regiment which consisted mainly of New England Blacks. After the Civil War, however, Africans had to pursue liberty in a different manner.

Renewed Fight for Liberty

The Emancipation Proclamation created official freedom for a large number of Blacks, but no immediate protection for that freedom. Some old troubles ended while new troubles began.

Large numbers of whites decided that Blacks would not pursue liberty peacefully. The attitudes of slavery still lingered in the minds of many whites, both in the North and in the South. This pseudo-racial democracy continued for approximately eleven years, before the political "horse-trading" between the South and the North crystallized during the presidential campaign of 1874-75. This point marked the beginning of the period that could be called the betrayal of the era known as Reconstruction.

During the last twenty-five years of the nineteenth century, Blacks in the United States were forced to begin again their fight in pursuit of liberty. Many Blacks who had been duly elected to public office were physically barred from entering some of the legislative halls in the states. The political gains of the Reconstruction era were lost. The late Professor Rayford Logan, formerly of Howard University, referred to this period as the "nadir"—symbolically the hour of our greatest depression.

African cultural continuity was more difficult to sustain in the United States at this point than it was in the Caribbean because African religions and the use of the drum were outlawed. Nevertheless, its impact could be seen in the work of the American Colonization Society and early back-to-Africa movements, such as the Chief Sam movements in Oklahoma during the 1870s and the movements led by Bishop Turner.

Near the end of the nineteenth century, whites who had shown an interest in the cause of Blacks grew tired of trying to communicate with a multiplicity of leaders. Finally white editorial writers and philanthropists of good will anointed a man they could accept as leader. His name was Booker T. Washington. As the founder of Tuskegee Institute, Washington came to public attention after his speech at the Atlanta Cotton Exhibition, which some regarded as an attempt to make peace with both the North and the South.

As an educator, he was misunderstood then, and he is misunderstood now. Many people regarded his political views as weak, but he was a great and an imaginative educator who taught and practiced self-reliance. They failed to assess properly his views and methods, which were both strong and beneficial to Black people in the United States and abroad.

This was the period when W. E. B. DuBois emerged as one of the finest intellects of African descent produced in the entire western world. It was also the period of Black radical journalists, such as T. Thomas Fortune and William Monroe Trotter.

The African movement in pursuit of liberty has had a worldwide influence. In the Caribbean, newly freed Africans were discovering the feeling of their emancipation, just as we had discovered the feeling of ours. In Africa, colonial wars were being waged as they had been waged for nearly 100 years, and Africans were discovering the feeling of their emancipation, just as we had discovered the feeling of ours. In fact, the pursuit of liberty by African people all over the world has brought us fighting, hoping and bleeding into the twentieth century.

The fight in the pursuit of liberty to which I have referred is only a preface. The rest of the story is a current event.

Dr. John Henrik Clarke
Professor Emeritus
Hunter College
New York, New York

Dr. Yosef ben-Jochannan

THE REAL STORY OF THE SCRAMBLE FOR AFRICA

The real story of the scramble for Africa is presented by major Western institutions such as Cambridge, Oxford and others as having started some time around 1830 A.D. when France invaded Cueta, the most northern part of Morocco closest to what will be today the Rock of Gibraltar. And from 1830 that scramble went on until 1864 and then again started in 1884 at which time the Berlin Conference was called by Otto Von Bismarck and Kaiser Wilhelm.

But that kind of analysis will be totally in error and the purpose of the error, if we want to call it that, was the Suppression Tax. The scramble for Africa did not take place at that time, neither did it take place when the so-called explorers of Africa came in, such as Mungo Park, Burton, Stanley, Livingstone and others, for that brings us to the 1800s or the nineteenth century itself.

The scramble for Africa took place before there was the first European power in history. I'm talking about before there was a Greece. The scramble for Africa took place before there was a book in the Bible called Genesis, because that is not until 1700 Before the Christian Era (B.C.E.). The scramble for Africa took place when the

15

first non-African people invaded Africa for the purpose of taking African land, that takes us up to 1675 B.C.E. when the Hyksos or the people called the Shepherd Kings came from around the Oxus River in Asia and invaded Lower Egypt or the Delta region. The Africans there were already into their Thirteenth dynastic period. The Hyksos came under the leadership of Saletis. The Hyksos were removed from Egypt at the end of what is called the Seventeenth Dynasty. This dynasty was started by Ahmose, and continued into the Eighteenth Dynasty by Ahmose's son, Thutmose I and grand-daughter Hatshepsut, then his great-grandson Thutmoses III. Thus ended the removal of the Hyksos from Egypt.

There was another period in which the scramble for Africa in ancient time took place, and that's when the Assyrians invaded Egypt under the leadership of Ashurbanipal, and that will bring us to about 714 B.C.E. About that time the Ethiopians were ruling Egypt, under the reign of Piankhi, and others. Following the Ethiopians came the Persians with Cambyses, who was quickly removed and replaced by Darius I. That will bring us to 525 B.C.E. You will be surprised to know that from this period, 525 B.C.E. with Cambyses, not one solitary African ruled Egypt at all until 1956 A.D. when an African-Egyptian of Sudanese parentage named Mohammed Naguib over-threw Farouk and established Egypt as an independent nation. Most people think it's Gamal Abdul Nasser, but Naguib ruled Egypt before Nasser and others removed him. Naguib was calling for the reunification of the Nile Valley, meaning Egypt, Sudan, Ethiopia and other nations joined together.

Between the period of the Persians and Naguib there were other invasions. The first time the Europeans came into Africa as conquer-ors was in 332 B.C.E. It was the Greeks with Alexander II, son of Phillip of Macedonia. This occurred after the Persians in 525 B.C.E. in what is commonly called the Thirtieth Dynasty. The Greeks were finally overthrown by the Romans under Julius Caesar in ca. 30 B.C.E. The scramble for Africa did not start in North-West Africa after Hamilcar Barca had taken the islands around Rome and marked out the Mediterranean, then called the Great Sea, or the Sea of Sais. After his ship was destroyed in a hurricane the Romans wanted to take back the Iberian Peninsula.

The Romans made an attempt to grab Khart-Haddas, which Western Europeans called "Cartage" (and today's Arabs "Tunisia"). The Romans were repulsed by Hamilcar Barca's two sons— Hasdrubal Barca and Hannibal Barca. Hannibal pressed on and went across the Iberian Peninsula, now called Spain, Portugal and Southern France, turned to the right across the Alps and literally down to what was called the "Gates of Rome." For ten years he remained there with his troops, attacking and defeating everything that the Romans could throw against him, only to be surprised by a traitor, an African, the kind that we so often see today—a man called Scipio Nasisca, or "Scipio Africanus." Why? For the same reason today. Scipio Nasisca wanted to go to bed with Hannibal's sister, the Queen. He had attended the same school with Hannibal and his brother, thus she knew him, and denied him. And so Scipio decided to sell his services to the Romans against his best friend.

That attack continued until Scipio Nasisca told them, "You don't defeat Hannibal on land; you can't." Hannibal had elephants which mowed down anything in their way. But around 212 B.C.E. instead of attacking Hannibal in Europe where he was, the Romans crossed the Mediterranean at Numidia, the state where the Great Reformer of the Christian Church was born. The man who made modern Christianity what it is today, the same used in England today. This African made Christianity what it is, I'm talking about Monica's son, St. Augustine, who gave the fundamentals of modern Christianity in his book, *On Christian Doctrines*. But they were unable to catch Hannibal, because Hannibal's brother, Hastrubal, was no good either! He got killed in a whore house.

The next scramble came by a group that came all the way from Germany through France, Iberia, and that was the time when Augustine himself was living in 430 A.D. That same year he died, Genseric came into North-West Africa. So you see the scramble for Africa went back for thousands of years before 1830 at Cueta.

So it is here at Cueta that wise men taught in the University all that I have just spoken of so far because, the universities have denied you from being Africans; because you don't understand all that they teach you. That's the problem. So when you read about the Carthaginians, the Ethiopians, the Nubians, the Egyptians and the people of Lebes or Libyans as they are called today, you have no concept that they are speaking about you, because the professors in Oxford, in Cambridge, Harvard, Yale, and in Berlin have removed you from being African to something else.

When we look at what they are teaching now and have not tried to suppress in certain areas, we need to go to an Englishman, Sir Edward Hertslet, the official historian of Queen Victoria. Hertslet wrote for Victoria a three volume work called *The Map of Africa by Treaty*, showing all of the so-called "treaties" that the British, French, and other European colonialists were supposed to have had with the Africans. In what language? And the Africans' signatures are there in English, and there was no such thing called the English language; yet he signs his name in English, such as Azingha-a-cum, the Emperor of Manikango. He was the king whose sister Nzingha, Queen of Matamba, fought the Europeans for thirteen years at the head of her troops. She was not different from a woman by the name of Kahina or Dahia who stopped the Arabs from coming to what is today Morocco, only to get time for her sons to become Muslims to protect her people. Her son, Gibral Al-Tarikh, is the one for whom Gibraltar is named.

Now we are talking before the Pope in 711 A.D. and later in an agreement in which Portugal is going to get "the eastern half of the world," and Spain "the western half." This will come later when the Pope in Rome divided the world between Spain and Portugal. The scramble now continues. The slave trade started to the West in 1506. Bishop Bartholomew de las Casas and Pope Martin IV of the same Roman Catholic Church got twenty-five cents per head for each African slave to save [his or her soul] so that if they died across the triangular trade they would go to heaven.

This continued until France came down, with England close behind, little Switzerland (landlocked), even tiny little Denmark was going to get colonies in Africa; a mad scramble. Europeans had gone mad. England was then dying from scurvy. France was also dying from malnutrition. They came out to every place bringing God with them. "God" is called "cannon and gun powder." Gun powder which was even designed in Germany by an African called Berthodus Schwarz.

Germany did not get her share, because Germany was fighting France for Alsace-Lorraine. Germany defeated France, took Alsace-

Lorraine, and now decided she was going to take some of the territories that other European powers and England had already taken. Of course, France and England took the lion's share. And England no bigger than a toothpick in comparison to other colonialist countries and the continent of Africa refused Germany's bid. And so what happened was, Germany started taking away the lands that her other European colleagues had already taken. By the time Germany grabbed Togo and Babatus (I'm sure a lot of you from Barbadoes don't even know your country's name is Babatus), I'm talking about the Cameroons, which originally was Babatus. It was there in 600 B.C.E. that Necho II, an Egyptian king, commissioned Admiral Hano to circumnavigate the continent of Africa. There was no England, and there was no France yet, and of course there was no Christopher Columbus to save the Moors, as he knew damned well the world wasn't flat; and that had nothing to do with his sailing to the West with an African pilot by the name of Pedro Alonzo Nino, captain of the Santa Maria, who carried Christopher Columbus—Christobal Colon—into the Atlantic Ocean long before that liar who got lost.

And so they called the Berlin Conference in Germany, at that time headed by Otto Von Bismarck and Kaiser Wilhelm, attended by the same United States of America who tells you that they had nothing to do with this scramble for Africa. It is the master lie of them all. At the Berlin Conference they gave another "Christian civiliser," King Leopold II, the biggest and richest half of Africa they thought at the time. Leopold decided to keep the whole of Mani-Kongo, which they later called the Congo Free State, more than many times the size of Netherlands and Belgium included. You could place Germany and the Netherlands in Mani-Kongo, carry it across the place with an airplane, and it would still not touch the borders. This colossal estate he wanted to exploit, so he travelled in Europe, to England, and all over the United States of America and started what they called the Congo Free State. They decided that it was here that "International Law" was going to take place. There were African nations at the time of the Berlin Conference in 1884-86. Haiti in the Caribbean Sea, Liberia in West Africa by 1847, and Ethiopia on the east side of Africa were not invited to the Berlin Conference. It was strictly England, and the twelve European states along with the United States of America. Thus when the United States of America says she had nothing to do with the "partition of Africa" she is lying, because the representatives of the United States of America at the Berlin Conference was John A. Kasson, and at the Brussels Conference, Edwin H. Terrell. Both of them carried the title minister plenipotentiary and ambassador extraordinary. You can find this in the second volume of Sir Edward Hertslet's official documents on the Berlin Conference and Brussels Conference.

King Leopold II had Mani-Kongo. The other powers started to realize that Leopold had got the best part of the deal and so they tried to steal it from him. Leopold therefore, called a second conference at Brussels; and there at Brussels the decision was made to start an international system of law to govern the world under the control of England and the twelve European colonial powers with the support of the United States of America which had by this time made attempts to take over Liberia. (These supposedly started on a humanitarian basis during the rule of President Monroe, after whom the capital of Liberia is named—Monrovia—after the establishment of two little colonies, Maryland and Monrovia. In 1847 the Africans who came back from the United States of America decided they had had enough abuse from these people who were supposed to bring them "into civilization" again. After the United States of America had given two naval frigates to mow down the indigenous Africans at home, those Africans who had returned from slavery in America eventually killed off their European teachers of civilization from America and established their own independent republic in 1847. Of course, later, France also tried to take over Liberia's customs on the pretext that Liberia owed her some money; and therefore she took control of Liberia's export and import.)

That scramble for Africa established the basis for Woodrow Wilson, the United States of America's President in 1918, to start another fiasco called League of Nations. After Kaiser Wilhelm and others had realized that they were going to be left out, they started fighting not only for Togo but also for Cameroons in West Africa and Tanganyika in East Africa. The Germans went to West Africa, then on to East Africa with Dr. Karl Peters and others, where they took Tanganyika. In the meantime a very sick man from Scotland suffering with tuberculosis, one Cecil John Rhodes, came to Africa to get better. An African woman came to his aid and gave him all kinds of potent medical mixtures Europeans called "witch doctor concoctions." They called it that, but it saved him. Rhodes was to survive and attempted to create what England wanted, the Cape to Cairo railroad, only to be frustrated by the Ethiopians and the people of Uganda, the Baganda Kingdom of that time which was still united.

You're talking about "holocausts?" Nobody bothers me with nonsense about "holocausts," because let me tell you about my "holocausts." Let me tell you what Cecil John Rhodes, Dr. Leander Starr Jameson and others did to my people in South Africa (Monomotapa) when they brought in Captain John Lugard, who made Hitler look like a sissy boy. Lugard was exterminating the Indians in India by the millions. They brought him to do the same in South Africa, and moved him from there to what was later called Nigeria Protectorate. I do not know why Nigerians do not change that stupid colonial name. Nigeria was a name that came out of Lugard's woman, Flora Shaw of the *London Times*' mind. She called it after the River Niger because he constantly wrote her about it; thus, she suggested the name "Nigeria." It's about time these Africans find a suitable name!

You are talking about holocaust and you forget the Congo where twenty-five million African souls were murdered during the triangular trade and another fifteen million were lost when African women found it revolting to give birth to a child under slave ship's barbarity, and so threw their children in the Atlantic Ocean to the sharks. It was a better fate than the slave ship and the slave plantation awaiting them.

That scramble for Africa, as Professor Clarke said, equally saw the destruction of ancient Ghana, for which modern Ghana is named, in 1076 by the Almoravids, or otherwise Almahodes. The destruction of the University of Djenne, which was more than a thousand years before the university that was copied in Salamanca, Spain, Europe's first university. University of Djenne was rebuilt as the University of Sankhore, in the city of Tombut, which the French later called Timbuktu.

That scramble for Africa was to continue even when the First World War, 1914-1918 A.D., was over, in which Africans fought for their masters' freedom, i.e. France, England, and everybody else but themselves. And when Kaiser was defeated nothing like "freedom" came to the Africans. We went and fought against Hitler to free England, France, and other nations of Europe. We stopped the bombs from dropping on Coventry and elsewhere. But the "freedom" that these people gained was not "freedom" for us.

That mad scramble for Africa went on until Dr. Kwame Nkrumah intervened in 1947 and fought the British until independence was won in 1957 for Ghana. Their guns could not lock him in. The scramble for Africa started to descramble itself, as Ahmed Sekou Toure told France to get out of Guinea. Charles de Gaulle was so upset that he even took the common toilet paper out of toilets in the French's attempt to destroy Guinea. And it was that night that the Osagyefo Dr. Kwame Nkrumah gave Guinea "twenty-five million shillings" otherwise Guinea would have begun its independence flat broke. It is a fact that England would not return the "pounds sterling" that she was supposed to give the freed colonies on the day of their independence, and likewise France would not give back the millions upon millions of francs that she held belonging to the Francophone nations.

There are several questions asked for Africa's present condition but the question is not overpopulation and trying to sell birth control devices in Africa. The question is unequal distribution of the world's wealth. The question is the control of the economic market thus, internationally forcing Dr. Kwame Nkrumah's Ghana cocoa and gold market into chaos. The question is not the Malvinas Islands of South America. The question is not the missionary coming into South America talking about something he or she doesn't know about. You don't come to preach Christianity when you haven't got "Christian compassion" yourself. You must first get yourself straight, then come to get me. I wish, in fact, we had eaten missionaries, as they said!

I end with a short Kwaku Ananse story, from West Africa. There was a missionary who came to Africa dressed in the usual attire, short pants and British colonialist hat; also a bag of everything and they would look at him and spit. Then he went into the forest to pray to Jesus. He said, "Jesus, I know you are still with me. You have not left me, you were just testing my faith." And just then a lion that somebody had shot came limping by his side. He said, "Jesus don't worry about it. I'll tell you, your words are always perfect. I didn't get the humans, but I got this lion." And so the lion sat down with his head and two front legs in the air, and said, while looking at the missionary, "Lord I don't know what he's praying for, but I'm thanking you, God, for my meal."

Dr. John Henrik Clarke

AFRICAN RESISTANCE AND COLONIAL DOMINATION: THE AFRICANS IN THE AMERICAS

The story of the Africans who live outside of Africa is more than a twice-told tale, yet their true history is basically unknown. There is a large body of literature on the subject, mostly written by able writers of African descent, that is still neglected. Yet theirs is one of the longest struggles against oppression in the history of the world.

The subject is always bigger than the time allowed to discuss it, so I will go straight to the subject. I have said and documented that we, as a people, have been under siege for over 3,000 years. We have been under siege for more than 3,000 years but let's be satisfied just to look at 3,000 years of siege as a preface to this talk. For at least that period of time our lives as a people have been plagued by people trying to take what we have, trying to extract our labor, our land, and our resources, and we have been under siege as people principally because we have always had and still have things that other people want, things they cannot do without, and don't want to pay for. And for 3,000 years the enemy has either been at the door, in the house or in our beds. Now this last item is cruel. It is cruel because when you study the nature of conquest the first thing the conqueror assumes that belongs to him are your women. And the first thing the conqueror begins to do is the bastardization of a people. When a people are bastardized there is set up among them a separate group within the group who are at odds within themselves about their loyalty. If I take this to its logical sequence, I will have to explain why that group kept Haiti from becoming independent, and literally kept Jamaica from becoming independent. When a people are not too sure about who they are loyal to and what their commitments are they represent a danger within the cultural mainstream of their society. This is what the Europeans did, especially to the Africans in North America, to the Africans in South America and to the Africans in the Caribbean. We have to understand the different nature of oppression the Africans in these three areas were reacting to, the historical experience over which they had little or no control, and how they became what the nature of their oppression made them.

I will have to take a broad view of the subject to let you see that resistance did not start with or during slavery or in the colonial period. First, we have to study the slave-buying customs of the European. In the United States they bought slaves in small lots and they resold the lot piecemeal. As a result, in the United States, Africans were separated instantaneously. When you separate people, break mother away from father, cousins from other relatives, you are breaking up the one thing that holds a people together, their loyalty system. In the Caribbean and in South America they generally bought slaves in large lots and kept the lots together, not out of kindness or humanity, [but] because they thought slaves could be worked better that way. They were right, they could, but the one item they forgot is that because the slaves remained together, and because some of them came over on the same boat, and because some of them came from the same region of Africa and therefore had the same basic culture, they could maintain their loyalty system. It was the loyalty system in South America and in the Caribbean that made the revolts in those areas more successful than the revolts in the United States.

Now, if you are thinking fast, you are probably thinking wrong. The Africans in the Caribbean and in South America were not one mite braver than the Africans in the United States. If they fought better and longer in their revolts, and if they were more successful, it is because the nature of the structure of their slavery permitted them to maintain a loyalty system, one to the other. If you look at the nineteenth century Caribbean African you will find a consistency of loyalty. Because the loyalty system had broken down in the United States the slaves held no loyalty, one to the other, and the major slave revolts were betrayed by house servants. In the Caribbean, the major slave revolts were planned by house servants and carried out by all of the slaves because the house servants and the people in the fields had not broken their lines of communication.

Let's go back a little further and look at the coming of slavery itself. This is an event in history that we have not looked at except to look at it and become depressed. The period from 1400 to 1600 was a turning point in the history of the world. In 1400 Europe was coming out of the lethargy of its Middle Ages. The Africans, the Arabs and the Berbers had been controlling Spain since 711, and they were still in control of Spain. Their control of Spain blocked the Europeans' control of the Mediterranean. That is part of what the Punic Wars were all about: control of the shipping trade in the Mediterranean, then the Sea of Destiny, and it would remain, for a thousand years, the Sea of Destiny because it touches on three continents and the control and the scramble was really for North Africa—that opening door to Africa, right at its top—and hinges upon the world's first major melting pot.

At this point in history, the Crusades were over. We won't deal, in detail, with the Crusades. If you were thinking they were religious wars, you have misread history. These wars were launched to get Europeans out of Europe. These wars served as emotional drains on Europe and as an outlet for the Europeans with a whole lot of pent-up emotions, especially against the church, to start marching and forget their anger against its judgments. They would not remember their anger again until the Reformation.

Between 1400 and 1600 some events happened that we need to pay some attention to. In 1415 the Portuguese, among other European nations, were living in fear of the so-called infidel Arabs. The Portuguese, who had been originally living under the domination of the Africans and the Arabs, freed themselves from their domination. They managed to free themselves from this domination because of an argument between two African and Arab groups, the Almoravides and the Almohad. In that year, a little known event in history occurred, the battle of Cueta. The Portuguese were lucky enough to successfully attack a little enclave off the coast of Morocco. This victory stimulated Europe into thinking that the infidel Arabs were not beyond defeat. This minor victory was seen as a major victory and helped Europe into getting its nerves back. It had had frayed nerves. It had literally lived, for hundreds of years, in fear of the Africans and Arabs who were blocking their movements in the Mediterranean. After the battle of Serta, the Portuguese began to assert themselves and this assertion would lead to the weakening of African and Arab hold on the Mediterranean. With this weakening, this argument between Africans and Arabs—dissension within the ranks of the controllers of Spain, led to about one-half of Spain becoming free of their domination.

With both Spain and Portugal becoming free and the opening up of new trade routes, in 1482, a point to be remembered because an assault was made by the Portuguese to establish permanent homes, the first one being Elmina. Elmina castle is still in existence and most of the castles along the coast of Ghana are still in existence. Now there is a scramble for footholds in this part of Africa, and this is literally going to become the headquarters for the slave trade. Back in 1455, the Spanish and the Portuguese had gone to the Pope to ask for lines of demarcation for areas they opened up. Everybody had to go to the Pope to engage in the slave trade, and the Pope would tell them rationally that, "You are both authorized to reduce to servitude all infidel people. If they are not Christians they are fair game for slavery...." He was telling Europeans to engage in the trade and that they need not feel guilty. England was out of it, at this point, because of a difference of opinion with the church. This difference of opinion with the church, literally, kept England out of the trade for its first hundred years, but she was the errand boy for those in the trade.

Now let's look at the significance of the year 1492. This year holds significance that the African should pay attention to. There was a little known sailor called Christobal Colon, later to be known as Christopher Columbus, who, if you read his diary, says, "As man and boy I sailed up and down the Guinea coast for twenty-three years." If you ask what Christopher Columbus was doing up and down the coast of Guinea for twenty-three years, the only answer is that he was a slave trader among other things. We know that Christopher Columbus, allegedly, discovered America. We also know that never did he set foot on North America or on South America. And if he did not do this, he discovered absolutely nothing. But what he allegedly discovered or what he allegedly did not discover is not what is important here. It just helps in trying to show how all of this got set in motion.

Your history books tell you that a major event happened in 1492, but something else happened within Africa in that year that Africans need to pay some attention to also. In 1492, Sonni Ali, emperor of one of the last great African nations in West Africa, Songhay, was drowned on his way home from a battle in the south. He had been an able ruler and his conflict with the priests was over religion. He was not a Moslem, but now with a year of interruption, a year when nobody was on the throne, there was a scramble for power and a commoner came to power, Mohammed Abu Biki Ituri. He was a devout Moslem. He restored the priests, the old Moslem preachers and the imams, to their former positions at the University of San-kore, and on his way to his inauguration the sister of the deposed king shouted out saying what he had done to her brother and calls him a foul word in the language of that day. She calls him this word in as many languages as she can remember. She calls him, throne stealer, usurper, thief. He stops to answer her and says, "I will not let the wailings of this sick woman disturb me. Henceforth this is the name of my dynasty, call me throne stealer, usurper, thief." He created the last of the great dynasties of the independent African nation-states before the encroachment of the slave trade that spread inland into Africa. He had been prime minister for thirty years and he had ruled the nation-state for approximately thirty-six years. In this, the last of the great African nation-states, Songhay covered a massive area larger than the continental limits of the United States. He ruled exceptionally well with ambassadors coming from all over the Mediterranean area and with one of the leading universities of that day. There were two universities in the world now, the University of Salamanka in Spain and the University of Sankore in Timbuktu. My main point in relating this is that while the slave trade was starting along the coast of Africa in inner West Africa a great nation-state was going through its last years.

After the death of Sonni Ali's successor, Askia, a man whose life needs far more treatment than I have time to give it here, the state began to be envied by the Moroccans and a black king named El-Mansuri II. Using European mercenaries, they sent an army across the Sahara to attack and destroy the state. He was successful. The largest and the last of the great nation-states in West Africa was destroyed and the structure of Africa had been shaken. The two catastrophes that had overtaken Africa over the 600 years of the Arab slave trade and the European slave trade had changed Africa for all time. There is something a scholar of this period must understand, whether they are Moslem or not, because it is true. Except for the drain of Africa's time and resources brought home by the Arab slave trade and the Arabs in general, Africa could have had enough strength and organization to resist the European slave trade. Because the Arabs who pursued the slave trade were only a branch of the religion, only people who used Islam as a rationalization for the slave trade.

By this time the slave trade is well underway. But it is mainly in the hands of the Portuguese and the Spanish and some Scandinavians. At this point, England is still out of the trade because of her differences in opinion with the church and King Henry VIII's sexual passion would literally lay the foundation for another church. He was not too successful with this, but the main thing accomplished is that England pulls completely out of the orbit of Catholicism and France is now in a position to sell her argument. France's King Francis, will now ask, "Show me the clause in Adam's will that says that I am not entitled to my share of the gold in Africa"—the black gold, meaning slaves. The Englishmen would cry out, "Who gave the Pope the right to give away kingdoms and peoples that did not belong to him?" Their attack was aimed at the church because the church was not only in the trade but the church had given orders to make sure that it got its proper share for being in the trade. There is no point in having slaves when you don't have a whole lot for them to do. But what would set the slave trade in full motion would be opening up the so-called New World, the extermination of the indigenous populations of the Caribbean and bringing in the Africans. Father Bartholomew de las Casas came over with Christopher Columbus on his third voyage, and it was Father de las Casas who went to Rome to convince the Pope to sanction the increase in the slave trade, to allegedly save the Indian population in the Western Hemisphere. He did not save any Indians. In fact when the Pope sent commissions to look into the conditions of the Indians, the Spaniards had no Indians left, they were all dead.

The Africans began to take hold of the Caribbean Islands. Some twelve to twenty-five million so-called Indians had disappeared and the Africans began to adjust. This does not mean that the African was beginning to adjust to slavery. He was adjusting to his condition and he was trying to see his way out of his condition and he is beginning some sort of resistance to his condition. This is the first record of slave revolts that I could locate, a record of a successful revolt in Cuba in 1527. Now these slave revolts would be continuous and intermittent for the next 300 years.

Besides the loyalty system that the slaves were able to maintain, there is another reason why the revolts in the Caribbean Islands were more successful and it is the same reason that they were successful in South America. The foliage, the mountains and the bush proved a natural advantage. This natural protection made the coming after them too costly. So in South America many slaves bypassed the auction block, went into the woods, were never slaves and founded an independent African community. The best known of these communities was Bahia, in Brazil, which still exists as a predominantly African city. Palmares, also in Brazil, was the most successful because it looked among its population and found Africans who were from the ruling class in Africa and made them a part of the ruling class in Palmares. At Palmares they had a defense system, and ways of finding the lineage of kings. This was an African state, the most successful of the African states in Brazil. Bahia was the most glamorous, but the one that was the most politically significant was Palmares.

The escaping Africans began using the space of the countries that they were in to their advantage. That fact that these countries were large and unexplored by the Portuguese was to their advantage. The Portuguese had not explored the mountains and forests and when the Africans escaped to them they extracted a toll of Portuguese lives that made any attempt to recapture them not worthwhile. The same situation was happening in the Caribbean, principally in Jamaica and a place at the northern tip of South America, which used to be called British Guyana. The area now called Surinam used to be called French Guyana. Many of the slaves in this area were from the same ethnic group. When an ethnic group remains together, they keep their language together and, most importantly, they keep their loyalty system together. A loyalty system that transcends language, religion and geography.

Let me explain what I am talking about. No matter where you are and no matter what religion you might belong to, and no matter what kind of schooling you have gone through you are distinctly an African person. You are a supporter of some loyal feelings for every African person that walks this earth and if you have confusion about that, you have confusion that is detrimental to the freedom of your own people.

The British entry into the slave trade made it an established business and gave it organization. They established spheres of influence that controlled where different nations could trade. They gave it the kind of organization that put it on a footing where the traders were constantly fighting with each other. England, because of her vengeance for being kept out of the business in its early stages, would literally drive the Portuguese out of West Africa. The Portuguese would then go down into Africa to the Congo and later to Angola and still later around to Mozambique.

My main concentration on what is happening to these African people away from home is that in the first part of the nineteenth century, in the Caribbean Islands, the British began to experiment with the concept of stopping the traffic at sea. Their concern had nothing to do with humanity, it had less to do with Christianity. It had to do with the business of the management of that kind of labor, and it had to do with the fact that a young nation, the United States, had studied the British ships and had made some better ships than the British had. The United States called their ships the Yankee Clipper, and these ships were outrunning the British ships at sea. The United States had been buying most of their slaves from the Portuguese and the Spanish and the English were going directly to Africa and coming back directly to the United States. The development of these faster ships by the United States was causing a threat to their ever increasing business.

If you think slavery in the United States was a business of the Southerner, you are thinking wrong and misreading history. The Southerner was a buyer of slaves and not a capturer of slaves. The part of the United States now called New England ruled the United States. It ruled what was called the United States then and it rules it now financially, culturally and otherwise, because that area had fashioned the states for free white Protestant males, middle class and up, those who agreed with the political status quo and for those who owned property and that is still the guide lines for the United States and its government.

After the war of 1812, a war that was really fought to stop the American competition with the English ships at sea, the English began to concentrate on the need to drain more wealth out of the Caribbean area, mostly from Jamaica. The Jamaican slaves began to mount one rebellion after another. While you know a great deal about the Jamaican Maroon revolts, that was only one of the many revolts of this nature. They were revolting continually. Before the Maroon revolts, Kofi, a house servant who came from Ghana, started a revolt [in] Guyana. This revolt is called the Berbice revolt. The first sea captain that came to the United States also from Ghana. Ghana was literally the headquarters for the slave trade. A lot of slaves came from Ghana, and those who did not come from the coastal area were held in forts close to the ports because these were holding stations for slaves until the ships got back to Africa. The situation reached a point where some of the Africans from certain parts of Ghana were so restless and rebellious that the word got back to the traders not to bring those Africans over here, they fight all the time. They were talking about the Ashantis from the upcountry of Ghana.

While international conflicts grew over the slave trade, the United States did not want to enter into the dialogue about stopping the trafficking at sea. The world listened to the phony abolitionists, the most famous and perhaps the phoniest were William Wilberforce and Granville Sharpe. There were groups of Black abolitionists in the West Indies and in the United States who were mounting these fights of agitation while the physical struggles were going on in South America, in the United States and in the Caribbean Islands. The first half of the nineteenth century saw the emergence of Haiti as an independent state. Jamaica had fought longer than Haiti, harder than Haiti, and Jamaica did not emerge as an independent state. This was principally because Jamaica was destabilized between revolts and the British made laws to outlaw revolutionary activity after each major revolt. But the Haitian revolt unfolded in a twenty-year period and not enough time was left to destabilize their revolutionary effort. Their consistent revolts were a fortunate occurrence in history because this fortunate occurrence brought off independence for Haiti, while Jamaica who fought harder and longer, but sporadically, did not get it.

My main point, as I conclude, is that throughout the Americas they had major revolts in the first half of the nineteenth century and that the African people were not liberated nor given any freedom. The British emancipation of the West Indies was a fake and the emancipation of the Africans in the United States was also a fake. So there is no point in saying that the slaves outside of the United States were emancipated thirty-five years before those in the United States because none of them were really emancipated and they are still to some extent slaves. By emancipation slavery was transformed, not eliminated.

I am saying that there is still something we have to fight against. Our brothers and sisters in South America and in the Caribbean and in the United States stood up against the slave system in this hemisphere while our African brothers and sisters were fighting a hundred-year war against colonialism. The caliber of the men, the caliber of their courage and the caliber of their character stands well in the history of the world and in the history of struggle of any people at any time in history. If we have to change tomorrow we are going to have to look back in order to look forward. We will have to look back with some courage, warm our hands on the revolutionary fires of those who came before us and understand that we have within ourselves, nationally and internationally, the ability to regain what we have lost and to build a new humanity for ourselves, first and foremost, and for the whole world ultimately. To do this we must extend the concept of Pan-Africanism beyond its original base to a concept of a world union of all African people, the African in Africa, the African in the Caribbean, the African in South America, the African in the Pacific Islands and, especially, the African throughout the world who has yet to realize that he is African too.

QUESTIONS AND ANSWERS

Q I'm not acquainted with the fact that there were any Europeans who were part of the Semitic branch. I recall what Dr. ben had to say, that Semitic comes from the terminology that means half, half-Asians, half-Africans and these people are not part of that stock, and, therefore, I cannot see how they can make such a claim. However, I would like to move on to the other question. I would like to ask our scholar to outline for me how much is the tactic used by European scholars, to disinherit the African community of the *Mystery System*. Secondly, Dr. Clarke pointed out the failure of racial identity in certain elements in our community. Would you give us a much clearer position on the fundamental danger of miscegnation because that is the catastrophic problem that we now have within the African community in this country. Thank you so much.

Dr. ben-Jochannan: I guess the first two were directed at me and the next to Dr. Clarke. I would answer the first two and if necessary assist him, and I'm sure he will add to what I say in the first two. I don't know if the statement you are referring to is in respect to Minister [Louis] Farrakhan. But I'm going to speak on Minister Farrakhan in spite of the statement made or not made. So I hope that you will understand that since I don't know the statement, I can't comment on it. Speaking in general, I do know that Minister Farrakhan was barred from entering England. That is my under-

standing from the television in the United States of America, and if
that statement is correct then I would ask the question: why did
England not bar [Israeli Prime Minister Menachem] Begin from
coming here, while there was British money on his head for the
bombing of English personnel and others in Palestine, which made
them withdraw an existing law that prohibited his entry on British
soil? They would have legally arrested him when he arrived here to
speak to Parliament. Minister Farrakhan has a right to interpret
history in whatever manner he desires, as anyone else in Great
Britain, including the Queen. Because if she interpreted history the
way I would like it to be, she would abdicate. Now let us go the
specifics of why they would bar Minister Farrakhan. Minister Farrakhan is supposed to have said certain anti-Jewish statements, or anti-
Semitic as is stated, understanding that Begin has no more right to
Judaism than I do. We both came from Jewish mothers, therefore
I am as Jewish as he is. I didn't feel offended by what Minister
Farrakhan said because there was no need, as he said the truth.
Hitler was a great man for the Germans. It was between 1933 to
1945 that Germans followed Hitler implicitly so they must have
thought that he was a great man. It's just like the Marxists saying
the "religion is the opium of the people." That wasn't even the full
sentence. Not that Marx is any nice guy in my books, because he
said some funny things about colonialism that I don't agree with,
but I'm not dealing with that issue.

About Minister Farrakhan having backed Reverend Jesse Jackson,
on the issue of "Hymie Town." Jews among ourselves in New York
call each other dwellers of "Hymie Town," so that is no big deal. It's
just that Jews didn't want anybody else to label them as such but
other Jews! The issue isn't Farrakhan; the issue is Islam. And because
Farrakhan has adopted Islam through the late Elijah Muhammad and
Malcolm X, there is a clamor to decide for Black people what we
must think; whether we are Jews, Muslims or Buddhists. European-
Judaism presupposes that it can speak for African people. I had a
debate on a television show not too long ago against one Rabbi
Seltzer, who came with the intent written in his papers to call me an
anti-Semite. But before he could speak I said to him, "Rabbi,
behold, I don't know what arguments you have. Since we are both
Jewish, the only difference is that I'm an African Jew and you are a

European Jew. There are things as an African I follow, Jew or not, and things that you follow as a European-American Jew or not. Not one Black person killed one white Jew in Hitler's Germany. I don't have to feel sorry for you, because you didn't come to Ethiopia when Mussolini was exterminating me, African Jews, in Ethiopia. My uncle went to the United States to the European Jews to secure some help against the Italians; and they gave him only $432."

So I'm trying to see what Minister Farrakhan said. Minister Farrakhan allegedly said that, "Judaism is a gutter religion;" his is too. He should know, it takes one to know one. And so why are they complaining? All that they should have said to Minister Farrakhan is, "O.K. we've got a religion, but you came out of the gutter too!" But they are so scared that they are not going to listen to Jews no more than white Christians or Buddhists. The whole thing is that they are so afraid of [Muammar] Qaddafi of Libya and anything he says, that they press anti-Semitic charges. This anti-Semitic thing is to stop anybody from criticizing anything happening in Israel and New York—"Hymie Town." The question I would ask is: what is Semitism to be "anti" it? I thought "Semitic" was a linguistic term; so am I anti-language? What the European Jews forget today is that they were as much involved with our slave trade as the Arab Moslems were, and as the Christians were. The Grandees did not worry about what they were financing the Spaniards for, to take us to the other parts of the West to enslave us.

What white Jews don't understand is that they are considered to be no different by Black people than white Christians, white Buddhists, white atheists, white anything else that involves themselves with our destruction. I live in Harlem, Central Harlem, I couldn't get more center, and almost every house that a Black person lives in a Jew left it for a Black person to move in the neighborhood. It seems like a Christian left it. There was a white person living in it; and white people behave like white people, bad, good and indifferent.

Lastly, I have stated before that under no condition will I marry a white woman. Let me explain; it has nothing to do with the white woman being inferior or superior. It has to do with the reality of the world condition. When a white woman gets pregnant by a Black man she is going to get a child, not a horse or a donkey. A white woman feels pain, cries, feels joy just like a Black woman. It has nothing to do with race, biology, and all that nonsense. It has to do with the reality. It has to do with the distinction of my race, and I didn't create that term "race." I'm going to struggle for my survival, and if I say that Black is beautiful and I'm coming to lead other brothers and sisters to the direction I'm going. I must realize that I must prove to the world that Black is beautiful. I will look like an ass walking in here with a white wife, talking about "Black is beautiful." For that reason anyone who wants to have one, that is their business. If there was a problem of snakes getting into my house and destroying my eggs, I will go and kill the snakes. When the snakes are no longer destroying my eggs, I will check which one is the grass snake, which is the copperhead, and which one is the brass head.

Can I lay in bed tonight with a white woman, then plan her father's murder and tell her: "I'm going to kill your father tomorrow?"

Dr. Clarke: What we have to understand in the broader sense is that people rise and fall within the context of institutions. There is an attack, a total attack on the cultural institutions of African people, and that's how we got into the trap that we are in today. And while we, not lacking an answer, permitted ourselves to be the world's whipping boys for other people. Now, if you look at the reaction of Europe towards the so-called Holocaust, they could have stopped it. If you go back and read the proceedings of the Evian Congress held in France; when they held this conference to do something about the Jews, England sent a British Nazi to represent her views, and so did France. They were all lying about helping the Jews and later the Jews were politically in bed with the same people who betrayed them. The Arabs had no gas chambers in those tents, and did not kill a single Jew. Europe always solves its problems at the expense of non-Europeans. If European Jews want a homeland they should claim part of Germany. But they won't do that. They will go outside to claim the Arabs' country that the Arabs a long time ago took from somebody else. In true historic terms it belongs to neither of them. The homeland of the European Jew is Europe. His problem was started in Europe by Europeans and should have been resolved in Europe by Europeans. He is mad now with the fact that the

Western world including people he is politically in bed with now turned their backs on him.

They knew exactly what was happening to him, and when it was happening the American and British intelligence knew exactly about these gas chambers, and there was no hue and cry. Now what we have to understand in the United States is that there are two hundred or more hate groups, all hating Jews at the top of the list. And these are paramilitary groups with arms and publications. Some own publishing houses and who will say categorically what they think, far worse than any Western army, far worse than anything Farrakhan ever said, and these people are going unattacked. Why are they using so many big guns on small talkers? Farrakhan has no army, he has no navy, no organization that can harm them considering their structure. During World War II, Americans were bombing Germany and parts of Europe, flew over all those death camps. One bomb could have destroyed a German railroad and they didn't even drop one. If you want to find your enemy do not look some other place. Look inside of your own European family, and look at the fact that you are young people. We were already old and you were a guest in our house and well-treated and you never returned a favor or sent us a "thank you" note.

This needs to extend to what happened with this invasion in 1675 B.C. When Africa was invaded, instead of helping African hosts, they became collaborators to the new enemies of Africa. When they entered Africa, they did not return the gratitude that the Africans had delivered to them; there was no acknowledgment of the friendship. And what we have to understand on a broader basis is that the relationship of Western people to non-Western people, from the destruction of Carthage to the destruction of Ghana has been a protracted act of aggression. It is hard for your mind to conceive. And as a Jew you are talking about a part of the Western world, and cannot be treated differently from any other people who have intentions to rule the world by any means necessary, principally, to rule us. If they have enjoyed the rise and fall of the so-called Western civilization, I'm talking about Europeans only now, during colonialism, they were just as colonialists as the others. During the slave trade they treated us just like any of the others, and in America they insured the ships in the trade. They were in Africa taking the diamonds and the gold long before the slave trade started. It was Africans who took them to Spain and protected them and when the Africans and Arabs lost Spain they joined the enemies of the Africans in the slave trade. Some went to Holland and founded a Dutch company that laid the basis of South Africa. Now we can talk about to what extent have they ever returned any favors to us. We are a people who never made good alliances. We are a people who have been historically and politically naive in our relationship with Jewish people, and once we deal with our relationship with Jewish people down through history, there's going to be enough embarrassment to go round for both of us.

Q I apologize for my impulsive disturbance, but the thing is I see the world differently. Everybody is entitled to see the world differently. If I were you, and I'm not, I would have six wives. First of all, and it may sound stupid, but the whole thing is, you are indoctrinated to have one and you won't have a white one, but you may have a Black one. I'm above all those things in my own way of thinking. I'm merely trying to prove a point by saying simply that as far as the different religions are concerned, I believe that Muslims are entitled to so many wives. And if one wants to reverse the situation in the case of the Caucasian woman, or the Negress, as you were saying that the white woman and the Black woman are both the same biologically and they both have feelings and so on, why not be brave and have three Africans and three white wives?

Dr. ben-Jochannan: I think the brother gave his opinion about things, but I guess he overlooked the qualification I made. I'm assuming that he overlooked it or he doesn't understand it, one or the other. He said based upon his condition, or position, and I understand that, too. You see I've got at least two heads, and the one up here rules the one down there. I particularly made the condition for my decision, and I carefully let you understand that I don't think that a white woman is inferior or superior, or anything like that. That's none of my concern. I also told you that we are at war, thus I am in a death struggle. When you are in a death struggle you have no time to be making jokes, or to be playing around to check skirts. I particularly gave you the scenario.

Let us look at the African heads of state who marry white wives, Cabral and others. Don't you consider what that African man was saying when he was fighting to gain control of that African country? Why is it that when the African man becomes head of state the African woman/wife isn't the First Lady? When Idi Amin was asked by a reporter, when his son was here, that he heard he was going to marry an English girl, Idi Amin responded that he, "didn't know Princess Anne or any of them in the British Royal Family was up for marriage. I am ready to marry. I am ready to marry a white woman when the Queen of England is ready to marry me. Nothing less, because I am as much a king as she is a queen." Am I going to marry somebody's secretary in England just to say I got a white woman! No way, you don't get the best for the least. So if you don't understand, this is a war; and a war is fought on every level. I know what sweet sex a Black woman could give you, and you will talk a lot of things you are not supposed to talk! Now I'm making the assumption that white girls would do the same thing, I don't know. I have never found the need to try, because I'm so happy at home. You see, as I told you before, brother; we have roses, there are all shades of roses. Why do I need to go to any place? I don't have the problem. I'm as comfortable at home as could be. But the most documented point is, I am not going to have any woman that when I plan to kill her daddy, she's going to hear me talking about it in my sleep and then tell him.

Dr. Clarke: I wish the gentleman will consider in his generosity and somewhat cultural naiveté that in Asia, there are probably about two million people called Eurasians, principally a mixture of English men and Asian women. There are not ten English men married to any one of them. In South Africa there are almost a million or so people called Cape coloreds. They came into being through the cohabitation of the English men and the Asian women and the African men and the African women. There is no English married to any of them. So you are generous and gentlemanly compared to what has been done to us and to our women.

Q The question goes to Dr. ben. I heard that the Jewish problem was going—Dr. ben to please clarify—were they initially going to set up the state of Israel in Kenya and Uganda, as I've read? What was going to be the justification for that?

Dr. ben-Jochannan: Well, you see, Zionism came out of central Europe, primarily, from a Jewish comedian. He wanted to speak to the Jewish people of central Europe. Theodore Hertzl started to present it to them in a comical manner. He first thought of Guyana, which was then totally controlled by the British. That didn't work out. The British weren't willing to part with any part of Guyana. They then considered Kenya and Uganda. The British were still controlling that. And the last thing they decided was to get South Africa. So Hertzl corresponded with Jan Christian Smuts, saying that if Smuts would grant them a homeland in South Africa, they would assist in the civilizing of the Africans.

That didn't work, and so the Balfour Agreement was conjured right here in London, while the Arabs were there in Palestine with a small group of European Jews, and some African Jews, as well as Asian Jews—all living in Palestine. But they arrange to double-cross the Arabs with a secret agreement called the Balfour Agreement, signed by Chaim Wiseman, an English Jew living in England, Jonah B. Wise, and Stephen Wise and others from the United States of America. And that made the basis for an agreement for the actions of President Harry S. Truman of the United States later in 1947.

I don't see why I have to say something else solely because I was born of a Black Jewish family. History is history, whether it's Jewish or not. I will not even call myself a "reformed Jew." I think I'm going to start calling myself agnostic and that will probably solve the whole thing. The only reason why I'm calling myself "Jewish" is because of a religious and cultural thing which my mother and father were born in, and that is the only reason about me now that one can call Jewish. I don't feel ashamed of it, some clean aspects of it, and I will deal with both aspects of it. I dropped it because I don't need it. Judaism came out of Africa, and not Africa out of Judaism. When there was not an Adam and Eve, or an Abraham, there was Africa. So my Africanism comes before my Judaism. I want this to be very, very, very clear indeed. There was a prime minister in England, a Jewish prime minister, who engaged in slavery, British colonialism, defended the crown and did everything to Black people in Africa and the Caribbean that he could possibly do as an Englishman. Because, you see, Disraeli was Jewish only when he prayed. Apart from that he was like any other English European. I don't know how much more rational or explicit we could be.

I can't for the life of me understand how it is we cannot see what is going on. I don't know whether the brother lives in an African neighborhood. Ten to one he does, unless he is escaping and you can't escape from yourself. What I suggest to the brother is a mirror test: a piece of paper, 8 x 11, lines or no lines, and a mirror and write what you see in the mirror and see if it comes out African or European. If it comes out African, then you have failed the jackass test.

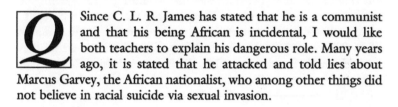 Since C. L. R. James has stated that he is a communist and that his being African is incidental, I would like both teachers to explain his dangerous role. Many years ago, it is stated that he attacked and told lies about Marcus Garvey, the African nationalist, who among other things did not believe in racial suicide via sexual invasion.

Dr. ben-Jochannan: I went to see Brother James. I think it was yesterday. I've talked with him and lectured with him in the same conferences. I read almost anything that I know he wrote. I am his junior of course, as he is a brother in his eighties; and I, as an African still respect age. As you noticed Brother Clarke is just about three years older than I am, but you equally noticed that when I sit here I always defer to him. If he wants to speak first, I let him speak first. We disagree sometimes; you should hear us arguing with each other historically and otherwise.

One has to understand what makes C. L. R., the man who wrote *Black Jacobins.* To understand C. L. R. I think you have to understand the period in which he came up. He is eighty-five years old, or more; C. L. R. came up with George Padmore and A. Sylvester Williams as Pan-Africanists. These men saw the freedom of the people and bolted towards Marxism. They had started as Christian young men, but Westernism and Christianity had failed them. They influenced Eric Williams to write *Capitalism and Slavery*. As a matter of fact, C. L. R. was Eric's direct mentor. And that was a marvelous historic work. He always believed he was right, deep, deep down.

But I can't accept communism, capitalism or Marxism. To condemn communism is to defend capitalism; but I think both of them stink. The point is that neither capitalism nor communism, nor socialism in my opinion was made for us. When [President Mikhail] Gorbachev and [President Ronald] Reagan sat down it wasn't on my behalf. They were discussing, "would we white people rule the world," or "which one of us will rule the world?" (By the way, let me clarify this; I'm not a member of the *third world*, I am a member of the *first world*!) So C. L. R., it was while writing for the American Communist Party, when he and Padmore and the others found out that at the time, the only way they could fight the system was in the communist movement. They thought that one of the ways to recruit a Black man was to give him a white woman friend and a lot of us fell for it. I could see all this; and I see all the errors they made. I feel that at this time C. L. R. James can't turn back and say he's made an error. Sometimes you can't teach an old dog new tricks, as I'm an old dog now. Sometimes I wish someone could teach me a new trick once in a while. But I've got some hard-held positions too, and I also can't be changed from that position. And I would admit that *Black Jacobins* and other works have made me what I am. His explanation of what happened in Haiti gave me a sharper view, and understanding. And yet, I can't accept his Marxism nor his white wife situation. But I don't want to throw the baby out with the dirty water.

Dr. Clarke: I have known and had associations with C. L. R. James even in correspondence long before I met him in person for over thirty years now. I think he's one of the primary intellectuals among Blacks of this country, which does not necessarily mean that I agree with him. I don't think anything is going to save us, except those things we devise ourselves. I don't think anything came out of the European control over the world, and that includes Marxism, to our benefit.

C. L. R. James is generous and idealistic on this point and we are tolerant and understanding of it while having strong disagreements with it. But I think he needs to be respected for the great contribution he made to revolutionize our thoughts among Blacks. I don't think he reached the point of understanding that, for a revolutionist, your personal life and your commitment must reflect that. He actually believed in the possibility of an integrated nonracial world, and if that is his belief we respect that without necessarily agreeing with it.

I think not understanding the cohesion that absolutely must exist between us is what has partly got us into traps. Other people have no qualms about facing this, and other people don't debate among themselves as to what they must do in regard to whom they should marry. They know that if they are going to survive they must walk this earth with the woman that looks like them. Let us continue to avail ourselves of the intellectual output of C. L. R. James. While some of us might disagree with him on the generous point of the ladies. But remember that he is more things than that and let us not forget his intellectual contribution to all of us. He is the last of the Trinidadian Pan-Africanists; the last of them alive.

Q Thanks to both of you. Dr. Clarke, we must have been on the same wavelength, because on the way here a brother and I had a discussion on what you summarized as sexual invasion and bastardization as a danger to the Black family. I would like you to speak on it, but before that we heard about polygamy. I was in Africa and when they talked about polygamy instead of more than one wife, it really meant more than one family. I hear marrying a bunch of wives, but I don't hear loving a bunch of wives. When you marry your woman, whomever you marry, please love her too, for that goes hand-in-hand. Now my question in terms of sexual invasion is, where do we go from here? Now, we have to deal with the results of not only the sexual invasion of when it was a man outside the race having relations with a woman in the family, but now it is women outside the race having access to our men. I need some direction on that, and also what kind of line is the coalition of politics that is coming up and how we may submerge what we want directly in line with what everybody else wants. Because there's a big thing going on in Berkeley, California, about that, and people are lining up against white men. I say that the first slavers of Black people are not white; Latins did it, and others who were not whites. So that is what I want both of you to address.

Dr. Clarke: The fact that there are people of mixed descent among us is a fact that we have to deal with. And all of them do not have divided loyalty, and different oppressors treated the situation in different ways. Like in Jamaica, there were separate neighborhoods for the browns and all those whites. In the U.S. our oppressors were more crude than yours. In fact when Europe dumped its human garbage can into the New World the worst of the lot came to America. We got the worst of the lot, and that lot took all those whites and browns, put them in one bag and put one word on the bag, and they all stayed in the same neighborhood depending on their economic condition. But it is time that we made some kind of truce or peace in this situation. Inasmuch as the European didn't accept his offspring, they have to end that confusion as to which house they need to go to. But if they come to our house we expect loyalty, and if they want to take their chance to go to their father's house, then they are taking chances. We know they are going back home, because we know that their fathers are going to accept them. And that's the cruel fact of history.

The event has already happened. You can't go back and undo this event, but we have to deal with it politically. You can look at how different parts of Africa dealt with it. In Sierra Leone it was a problem. In Ghana it wasn't a problem because the mixed ones declared allegiance to the unmixed one. Here's where nearly every single mixed Ghanaian, mostly the offsprings of missionaries cohabiting with Ghanaian women, every single one of them declared loyalty to the mother side of the family, worked for the rest of their lives showing this, and was hard and experienced as the blackest of the Blacks. This thing operated in different ways in different places. In the Black colleges of the United States, some of the earliest colleges were erected for those mixtures who could not go to native American schools and didn't want to go to Black schools. The restriction of American laws made them want to go to Black schools or no schools. Some of them became as loyal as the blackest of Blacks and some of them were confused not knowing which way they were going to go, one way or the other. But slavery and oppression left us with these problems. It's not going to be solved by whites. We are going to solve them, and the best way to solve them is on the basis of loyalty and commitment; who is committed to our cause, our ultimate liberation and nationhood and who is not. That's the only dividing line that I can lay down, the only criteria that I can lay down to judge those who have some confusion as to whether they belong to us or do not belong to us.

Dr. ben-Jochannan: Both questions are no problem to me, because I've lived through them. My father was married to my mother after his first wife died. My grandfather, my father's father, had sixty-three children with eleven wives. So I know what polygamy is as against promiscuity. The African tradition of polygamy is as respectable. There is such a thing as committing adultery in polygamy. And a lot of people think that polygamy is just jumping on a woman's stomach and acting-up like mad. That's promiscuity. Polygamy has definite rules of behavior and each woman is the head of her house in terms of her children, but all the women relate to the husband, the man, as the head of the family. But she's independent apart from that. She raises her children the way she sees fit, and when she can't handle them she calls the man, her husband. I think the missionaries' report about polygamy has made most of us condemn it.

I have nine biological daughters, three sons and eight adopted daughters, making a total of twenty children. I wish I could get more, because I'm an African, and I have no qualms about having a little tiny minuscule family called the modern family. I told my daughters that there's nothing wrong with polygamy. You want to marry a man with five wives, okay, but you must be a wife by the marriage tradition of the land. It is not as if the wife moves, and the girlfriend can move too! All the children of the various wives can come to the house and there is none that inherits and the other doesn't. A child was a child in Africa until the European came to mess it up with words like "bastards" and "illegitimate" garbage.

These are reasons why I say I've got to have an African woman. I've got to have somebody who understands me culturally. Because the European men keep their wives as a piece of furniture in the house, and she's got to rebel against him, as she is competing against tennis balls, gold balls and skiing down the Alps. The African woman has always had to work and there is no fear of the African woman taking over her man. They will never do that. They are always ahead of the men; we want them there. They are the sharpest minds in our business. I don't care if my woman doesn't love me, as long as she *respects* me. *Respect* is higher than love. Love is an animalistic thing which you have no control of. I must live the life before I can preach it. I have been married to an ex-Roman Catholic nun, a Black woman, and all the Jewish people on my side also said it couldn't survive, and yet we have been married for thirty-nine years because I respect her. I have so much time to praise and worship Black women, to kneel down and thank the heavens they are here!

 I read *Black Jacobins* when I was really young and the impression it made upon me was that it was not written by a Black. I was brought up over here, and I was reading a lot of white novels.

Recently I went to see the play, *Black Jacobins*, I came out of that play, having become much [more] knowledgeable in the intervening years, feeling quite convinced that the services C. L. R. James did were services to the white people who were actually trying to suppress us. I understand that Dessalines, the Black so-called slave—and they were not slaves, and this is why they revolted—that Dessalines was a tactician who defeated those armies. But on the stage, at the Riverside Studios, I saw Dessalines presented to me as a savage. And eventually this savage was further presented to me as having been taught how to behave by a whore. I saw Touissant presented to me first of all, as a weakling and then somebody who once he had taken over spent all his time in a white woman's bed. Now this is the play that was presented in C. L. R.'s name.

Christophe, who eventually ruled Haiti, was presented to me as an idiot. He said nothing on that stage. I know the direction does make a difference, but the direction comes from what is written, and ultimately the play ended like this. Dessalines, the great general said, "No more of the French. We will call this island after the name of the people who lived here before, Haiti." And the minute he said that he went on to add, "I want to be emperor," and that was the end of the play.

Now my contention is, I believe C. L. R. James had a great mind, and I will not take that away from him. He did his research, wrote it up and called it *Black Jacobins*. The Jacobins were white people in France. I believe that when he wrote that play his research was all based on his beliefs, if you like, in the whole Western academics that he used, and I will not take away from C. L. R. James his abilities, but I will say to you that he was totally confused and the service he did was to maintain the enslavement of our minds, and we have not had the tenacity and the time and the space to find out what was true about our heroes.

Dr. ben-Jochannan: When I went to see C. L. R. yesterday I must admit I didn't know he had written a play on *Black Jacobins*. I was surprised when I saw the poster. Remember I said I had great reservation and respect for Brother James. Having read it and having a background of the Haitian Revolution I could see why he wrote as against what you have seen from it. We see things differently. I think that shows C. L. R. missed the point of the conclusion. You see Toussaint was not the hero. That's why I said that it depends on the information. Let's go down to the Haitian revolution. The man that started the Haitian Revolution was Makandal, or Neg Yosef. The man that carried it on was Boukman. The man that started the actual action in the open was Boukman and the man that led the actual troops was Jacques Dessalines, who had already gone to the British colonies to fight in what became the United States of America with some other Haitians to conquer with General Lafayette. Why Toussaint got the credit was that he was trained by the Catholics and was Catholic as against being of the Voodoo faith. He had understood the French to the point of teaching French, and being French. But that didn't diminish Makandal, Boukman, Dessalines or Christophe.

For me the hero of it all in terms of the modern aspect of the revolution was Christophe. Christophe did the right thing. He should have killed off the whole of Santo Domingo. So now you can understand that I have problems with C. L. R. James, yet I know that there is some sharp part of the revolution which C. L. R. James covered that nobody else covered. But I am not a lover of C. L. R. James, and I still repeat what I'm saying again. When you look at the three of them together, they come to the limelight together with the Pan-African Movement. When Dr. Blyden put out his "Africa for the Africans" to which Garvey added "those at home and those abroad...," let me qualify myself so that you can understand me. C. L. R. James talked about Garvey like a dog, but it didn't make me stop and not recognize the other aspects of C. L. R. James' scholarship, because *Black Jacobins* isn't the only thing he wrote. If the conclusion of that play and the statements that you make is correct, then it's about time he be defiled. But sister, I guess I have never appealed for a man for understanding as C. L. R. James and that is because I had many occasions to work with him.

In the sixties they had a thing in the West called the Black Liberation Movement. We were in Bermuda where the Black Power Movement had moved for two world conferences. The British government sent the British marines. I wasn't part of it, because I don't join many things; but they were locking up and arresting the brothers and sending them back to the United States, including a member of the Bermuda Parliament. You may remember him, Brother Roosevelt Brown, who told the Queen where to go on the floor of Bermuda's Parliament, and he wasn't being nice. I was at the conference. I had camouflaged myself to get through. But when that man Nathan Wright (head of the Black Power Movement) was to show up to give the main lecture failed to turn up, C. L. R. James, though very ill, got up (I was a witness to this) and said, "God damn communism and any other 'ism,' I'm an African and I'm going to speak if Wright wouldn't come." He forgot communism, accepted that he was an African, but he had a warped way of showing it in terms of his own marriage. The same reason that deterred Wright from being present because he was marrying his white secretary. There are very few people in the situation of C. L. R. James that I ask consideration for; and yet he was Trotsky's secretary here in London. So when he was a young man at the time when his mind was being formulated, he was here trying to fight the English in England. He was frustrated when they didn't take him back to the Soviet Union. He has problems in those things and thus

I cannot make any kind of apology for the play. I have not seen it and never read it; and if it is that way, then I'm sorry for him.

Q What I want to talk about is that as a Black woman here I think we have a serious problem with the shortage of Black men. Now those they haven't succeeded in killing, they have got them in prisons, in the mental institutions, walking around not really knowing what they are supposed to be doing. Now I want to propose tonight, and I want both the men and the women to listen to this, that we grab our Black men and make them responsible so that they do not leave a child here and leave a child there and burden the Black woman; because when you have to work and support a child in this country or live with one or two children on social security, you are burdened, you are more than burdened. So what I want to suggest is that we start pulling our economic resources together, and that may be, I don't know what the division may be, five or four Black women have one Black man and we have him in the house; and that if he works, that money comes in the house and those children who live with us, let those men know those children. We can lie about this and lie about that, but in our hearts we know these children are all over the place. If we have that one man in the house, we have every single thing he works for, and we work for. We can start to build a family unit in recognition that there is a shortage of Black men in Britain. Any Black sister here who can say that she has one Black man to herself, I want to see him, because I'm sure another sister here can tell you it isn't true.

This is revolutionary talk and we are fighting a war. I would like to ask the wisdom of our elders on the possible way of some of us moving forward. It isn't going to suit everybody, because some people want to lie and tell themselves something other than reality. But if we are going to deal with reality, then we are going to have a chance to actually survive.

Dr. ben-Jochannan: You know it is not unique in England, my dear. In Harlem we have the same problem, and I will say the Harlems of America. I revisited the Virgin Islands. I spent some years there. I lived between Puerto Rico and the Virgin Islands and for years my mother lived in Puerto Rico. In the United States of America the things you say, the drugs, the jails and so on, and the other woman outside the family have dissipated the source of Black men. There's no doubt about that.

We also have the welfare department doing their share. If you are married to a man and he gives you a tough time, they chase him. But if you have a boyfriend, you get help. So what a lot of women are doing is chasing the husband and telling them to live in another place so they can get help from welfare. Then in the night he comes in and visits. Your solution is a logical one, but it can't be accepted because of conditioning, and the other sister cannot accept your position because again, what you are saying is to legalize polygamy and they can't deal with it.

There is another thing in the United States of America: Boyfriend X wants to date Girlfriend Y; Girlfriend Y has two children and hides them, so that Boyfriend X doesn't know. I think that I can't tell you to have a child and abandon it. I told my sons, the first one of you who abandons his child, I will get a junkie to blow your brains out. You see, you have to deal with the little brother in the house and get to that little brother to let him know. There is nothing wrong with sex. I enjoy it, can't get enough of it sometimes; but there is a thing called condoms, there are different types of them, and I don't have to prove to anyone that I am fertile each time I have sex with a woman.

Sisters, don't get pregnant for just anybody, get pregnant for a special somebody. Any male can make a female pregnant, but any male is not a man. I'm saying to mothers that we have not sat down our sons and told them about the respect of women like their sisters, and like their mothers. We sit down our daughters; but when they get pregnant you put them out of the house. We are afraid to speak to both of our children in the formative years when that African boy would understand the precious value of that African girl. I see it happen on the college campus, sisters dropping out of school because they are pregnant. Now somebody is going to tell me, why don't you tell your brother? Sister, we are dealing with a realistic situation. If brothers are walking out and leaving sisters, you tell the brothers and everybody about it. Then the sisters can no longer depend upon him that he is going to get intelligent. She has to protect herself. I told my daughters that: "If a man tells you he wants to carry your books from school, it isn't that he wants to carry your books, because he is not carrying his own. He wants to carry you to bed. Now you can't afford to get pregnant before you get the ring." What I tell my daughter is how to avoid getting pregnant. I've got to carry her to the gynecologist and tell him "get her ready for Freddie." Now you know that the men are not going to take no operation. You know it and I know it. Their ego will not permit it. So what I will say is, don't let the brother run any jokes on you, protect yourself until you are satisfied that this man is the type of man you want for yourself; don't get pregnant. That's all there is to it.

Dr. Yosef ben-Jochannan

THE AFRICAN CONTRIBUTION TO TECHNOLOGY AND SCIENCE

I will first express my appreciation for your having me here, and ask that you meticulously follow my comments, because as you know I'm known to be controversial, and that's an understatement. I'm controversial not because something is wrong with my documentation, but because I challenge Western hegemony.

Africa, as the label of my talk, cannot be spoken of in terms of Adam and Eve, because long before they had an *Adam and Eve* there was an *Africa* and *African* people, with concepts that predated Abraham. All of the pyramids of Africa, not only those in Egypt, but those in Sudan, and the two in northern Ethiopia (which the British and the Berlin Conference removed and put into southern Sudan), were built thousands of years before there was an Adam and Eve mentioned anywhere on the planet. When you get to the birth of Abraham, at the time when the Africans along the Nile are already in their thirteenth dynastic period, there is no Adam and Eve, because the Hebrews gave you the concept of Adam and Eve. Most of you believe that it has something to do with facts, rather than theocracy.

To speak of Africa you would have to revise your concept of the Virgin Mary and understand that it's nothing but a copy of Isis, and her husband God Osiris. You will also have to go to the Nile Valley to the temples there and see that this is thousands of years before Westminster Abbey, and, of course the Vatican in Rome. You can go all over the Nile Valley and elsewhere, and I use the Nile Valley, particularly, in that the oldest records of man are still there in terms of monuments. Of course, there are a lot stolen from Africa here in London, and in Berlin or other such places.

Your ancestors gave to the world the calendar in 10,000 B.C.E. (before the Common "Christian" Era). That is, 7,000 years before Adam and Eve. Your ancestors revised that dating system because of their understanding of the astronomical calculations. It is the science of astronomy that gives the ability to read calendars. Thus 10,000 B.C.E. saw the first calendar. The term is self-explanatory, the solar calendar showing the relationship of the moon and the sun, etc. that gives us the basis of the present calendar, with 364 days corrected each year, instead of 365 days corrected each fourth year. And I will say again that there wasn't a single European society in existence at that time. The first European writer, Homer, had not been born yet. And when Homer was born and finally became literate because of the teachings the Africans gave him, he too started to corroborate the evidence your ancestors had by stating that even the gods of Europe, Greece, in particular, which was then called Pyrrhus, came from Ethiopia.

I'm sure that those of you who have been to college, if not here in England somewhere else, know that I'm quoting from two works of Homer, the *Iliad* and the *Odyssey*, which brought Europe and England into civilization. The African we must talk about is the African that caused people to understand science, medicine, law, engineering, etc. It is common at the universities here to deal with science as if the art of medicine came from a Greek named Hippocrates. We don't have Hippocrates until about 333 B.C.E. Yet we don't need any record other than Hippocrates himself to know that what is being taught at the universities here are lies.

One has to realize that Hippocrates himself, in what is called the Hippocratic Oath, wrote that he had a god named Escalipius, the Greek name for the God Imhotep. Imhotep had died 2500 years before the birth of Hippocrates. Imhotep is the first known multi-genius other than the one you call Michelangelo. We don't have Michelangelo until 1609 and he is not known until he does the work of Pope Julius II, who commissioned Michelangelo to paint the ceiling of the Sistine Chapel. Michelangelo used his cousin and other relatives as models for some of the biblical characters that he painted. The basis of engineering was created by Imhotep. He created the first stone structure; that building still stands in a place called Sakkara, about less than an hour north-west of what is today called Cairo. And here you will see the Grand Lodge of Djoser at Sakkara. That modern structure was built in the Third Dynasty, since Djoser was the third pharaoh of the Third Dynasty. Imhotep was the man who gave us the little quip, "eat, drink and be merry for tomorrow we shall die."

The FIRST WORLD western university was the University of Jenne of Timbuktu. But as we continue, we realize that in the universities here you use paper to write on, and if it was not for paper the means of communication would not be as it is today. But in Egypt, Sudan and other such places, and I will remind you that Egypt is still in Africa, the Africans reached such a height in engineering that we even turned the Nile in an *S-turn* to cut down the flow when the inundation period came. That brings us to 2200 B.C. That means at least 1400 years before the first European wrote anything.

Africa, Mother Africa, as I prefer to call her, understanding that the Greeks called her Africa in about 500-400 B.C. I'm talking about the time when the first Greeks who had gone to Pyrrhus, who had come into Egypt by way of Leba (now called Libya) and established their little villages in a little enclave, they then called Africa long before the continent was partitioned by the colonialists. I am speaking about 11.3 or 11.5 million square miles of land, where first the concept of a God and Goddess Nut is shown as the mother of the sky. Symbolically, the God Geb, the god of the earth, lived in a little chapel in the center of Hathor. The African woman is giving birth even to the sun, in the morning through her vagina and receiving the sun back in the evening through her mouth. This shows the whole rotation of the world, long before the world had a beginning and an end. These Africans along the Nile were to do more of this.

They were to give us a God Osiris, where people went yearly to pay pilgrimage long before there was a wailing wall in Palestine or a myth of a Jesus born in Bethlehem, which changed at the Nicene Conference of Bishops, ordered by Constantine and removed from a cave in Ethiopia to a manger in Bethlehem.

It is Africa that gave birth to Hadzart Bilal ibn Rahab, who taught Mohammed ibn Abdullah, who was illiterate in his own language, not able to read and write. In spite of what your belief system may be, Hadzart Bilal ibn Rahab, became the head of the Moslem embassies under Mohammed ibn Abdullah, Omar the Great, and Abu Bakr. I think that we need to know history before we can quote texts in religious scriptures.

There was a myth of Africa as the home of a people who ate each other and missionaries. I wish we did eat the missionaries, it's never too late! We've got to understand that this Africa we are speaking about even established Europe's greatest universities and first, the University of Salamanca in Spain. The Africa we are speaking about produced the ancestors of the present Queen of England, George III, the German king who spoke no English. We forget that Elizabeth's grandparents and ancestors are related to George III, who was the son of Alexander the Medici, the cardinal of Rome who later became Pope, and an Ethiopian woman by the name of Martha. So I have to say, don't worry too much about it because Elizabeth belongs to the family. The Africa, which you may not know, happened to give birth to Zinjanthropus Boisei by the Africans of Kenya. The Leakey family, Louis and Mary, dated him to 1.7 million years old. Adam is about 4000-5000 years. The Africa you do not know gave birth also to Lucy in Ethiopia dated 3.2 million years old; they are both in Kenyan and Ethiopian museums. And some of us are still ashamed to be Africans! Some of us pay money to have our nose reshaped, our hair fried and boiled and all sorts of things, because we don't know this Africa; we know the Africa of the slave trade with John Hawkins from London and the other little songs.

Yes, that is the phase of Africa. Surely, slavery is a phase of lives past, but slavery is a tiny little bit from 640 A.D. with the Arabs,

1506 A.D. with the Europeans to now as against what I'm talking about; it is minuscule by comparison, because if I wished to go back to Africa, not only when we were performing astronomy, engineering in establishing the pyramids and so forth, but when we gave to the world the fundamental moral concept, "I have not killed man or woman." This is a response to the admonishing of the Goddess Maat. You notice that every time we talk about justice and rights we have an African woman representing the scales of justice. The response to the admonishings which would have stated, "You shall not speak ill of your mother and your father; you shall not kill man nor woman; you shall not hide a light under a bushel," sounds familiar to you because they said some guy named Moses discovered them thousands of years later on Mount Sinai.

Yet they said Moses was born in Goshen. This is the Goshen in Egypt according to the Torah or the Old Testament in the Book of Exodus. Moses had to be trained, and if he was born and lived there (for between age one to eighty-give years of age), according to your Bible, then he must have read this, because he was taught in the Grand Lodge. If he went to the lodge at age seven as a young boy, then he did not come out until he was forty seven, because it took forty years of training to make a priest in all of the disciplines. So then, Moses came as nothing but a copy of the Egyptian priests and Teachings of *The Egyptian Mysteries System*.

These same Africans went on to give us the concept of the monotheistic deity. Thus it was that Amenhotep IV, who changed his name to Akhnaton, who gave us the concept of a solitary god by the name of Aten. Akhnaton died long before the birth of Moses. Is it possible for you to come to England, go to kindergarten here, go to elementary school, college, do post-doctoral work and never hear of the English national anthem, the Magna Carta, or Queen Anne's statue? It is possible, just as it was for Moses to be born in Egypt, a soul brother, because his first wife was Deborah, according to the Bible, and never heard of Akhnaton.

And it is said that when Moses was running away from the Pharaoh for committing murder (before he got the rod on Mount Sinai), and his brother Aaron was charged for stealing from the Pharaoh's treasury, he met Deborah. It would seem to be that Deborah said, "That Egyptian," pointing to Moses; there was nothing in Moses to tell that he was Jewish; he was not wearing any special clothes; he looked like any other soul brother you can find in London, the Caribbean, Nigeria, Ethiopia, Ghana, the South Pacific. And then you say you are the minority! You are members of the third world. I am not a member of the third world, I am a member of the first world.

When one of the first of the so-called philosophers came to Egypt, we see him before 640 B.C.E. When he was supposed to have released his philosophical thinking, he is in Egypt. From Socrates down to Aristotle, the so-called post-Socratian philosophers, every one of them spent several years in Egypt and of course the only one who couldn't come since he was the creation of Plato's mind, was Socrates. And even he (Socrates) was supposed to have taken the hemlock for teaching African philosophy: "Socrates is an evil doer" was part of the charge against him. Plato had to run (and all the others) for teaching this philosophy. Would you have to run from England for teaching English history? Neither would the Greek government persecute the Greek philosophers for teaching Greek philosophy. It was somebody's philosophy they were teaching, and where did they go to school to know whose philosophy?

It is not until the Persians in 525 B.C.E. allowed them in, and it was not until 323 B.C.E. at the death of Alexander, the son of Philip of Macedonia, that Aristotle was allowed by General Soter (who changed his name to Ptolomy I) to have Tusak to bring those works down, that the Greeks had access to Egyptian works. Those who could study in Egypt for themselves did so, while some were sent over to Greece where they established what they called the Peripatetic schools in what later was called Alexandria, out of African materials.

Is that the African you know? It couldn't be, otherwise you couldn't be praising your masters; you would be going back to your educational past and be your own master, at least if not physically, mentally. It is difficult, because colonialism brings to us a kind of history written by the conqueror for the conquered to read and enjoy. When the conquered looks around and finds that even God speaks from the heart of the conqueror, the conquered then becomes suspicious of God. What is God's interest in all of this? It is not the African who said in the Songs of Solomon, Chapter 1,

Verses 1-9, and when you get to 8 and 9, it says, "Ye daughters of Canaan look not upon me because I am black, because I'm beautiful. My mother put me in the vineyard, but my sister, she kept indoors," that is why the Queen of Sheba turned black. I thought it was because her mother and father were black! But even in the Bible you find lies, racism and all that. As if we didn't have Bibles. We have "The Book of the Dead" which was changed right here in London from its original name in 1895 at the British Museum. It was called "The Book of Coming Forth By Day and Night." We have the "Book of the Divines," "The Book of Judgment," "The Heart of Judgment," and other such works, that preceded the Old Testament and the Jewish Kabala by thousands of years.

The Africans gave us the concept against murder. When the Shipwats at the Temple of Philos, a Greek word, which means Angelica, by the way, of the Goddess Auset, which the Greeks called Isis, and her son Heru, who the Greeks called Horus, and all the gods viewed the murder of Osiris by his brother Seth. A murder that preceded the Cain and Abel murder by thousands of years, beginning on the island of Angelica, continuing at the Temple of the God Horus, continuing further and you see the Virgin Birth and Immaculate Conception. It is here long before you see it in lifestyle, and you can see in life-size the drama that preceded Greece, showing Horus killing his uncle for the revenge of killing his father, showing his uncle symbolically as a hippopotamus.

This continued to the Temple of Osiris in Abydos, where pictures of the Virgin Birth, the Resurrection, showing Osiris' penis perpendicular to his body, being symbolic to the resurrection. When you go there you will see it all over the place. Those of you who have been to Egypt know that life is shown as the penis coming out of Peta's navel, representative of the extension of the umbilical cord, which is the extension of life, the source of life.

The Africa that I have spoken of, you need to know, and no one can keep you a slave after you know it. In America there is a saying that the mind is a terrible thing to waste. It is said on television all the time by people who call themselves "The Negro College Fund." You can only waste your mind on that one, and by using the term "negro" it indicates they've got no minds, because I have been looking for a negro, and I haven't found one in umpteen years.

Because I'm not a Portuguese, I don't create negroes nor Negro-land. I'm an African, and that word we need to deal with as having come from the Greeks. I guess some say it has got good connotations. So I beg of you to always carry a mirror, whether you are a man or a woman, to look at yourself daily. Then you've got to have a good feeling about that face you've got, the texture of hair you've got, and all the fine features you've got. I don't know about you, brothers, but when I look at the face of that African woman, I see heaven!

Dr. John Henrik Clarke

THE AFRICANS IN THE NEW WORLD: THEIR CONTRIBUTION TO SCIENCE, INVENTION AND TECHNOLOGY

I n this short talk on a subject that has many dimensions, and a long untold history, I am really talking about the impact of African people in the opening-up of the Americas and the Caribbean Islands. The appearance outside of Africa of African people in such large numbers tells us something about the greatest and most tragic forced migration of a people in human history. The exploitation of African people made what is called the New World possible, and the African's contribution to the sciences, invention and technology that made this new world possible, is part of a larger untold story. In the United States alone there is supporting literature and volumes of documents on this subject.

We need to examine the events in Africa and in Europe from 1400 through 1600 A.D. This is a pivotal turning point in world history. This was a period when Europe was awakening from the lethargy of its Middle Ages, learning again the maritime concepts of longitude and latitude and using her new skills in the handling of ships to enslave and colonize most of the world.

Europe recovered at the expense of African people. African people were soon scattered throughout the Caribbean, in several areas of South America and in the United States. A neglected drama in the history of dynamic social change had occurred in the year 711 A.D. when a combination of Africans, Arabs and Berbers conquered Spain and ruled the Iberian Peninsula for nearly eight hundred years. The aftermath of the African-Arab loss of Spain and the Arab's use of European mercenaries and equipment wreaked havoc throughout Africa and broke up the independent nations of inner Western Africa, mainly Songhay. This drama had to play itself out and the power of the Africans and the Arabs had to decline before the larger drama of the slave trade and, subsequently, colonialism could get well under way.

Africa was now suffering a second catastrophe. The first catastrophe was the Arab slave trade, which was totally unexpected, and came over six hundred years before the European slave trade. The second catastrophe was the Christian slave trade which started in the fifteenth and sixteenth century. Early Christians could not deal with what African religions were before the advent of Judaism, Christianity and Islam nor could they deal with early Christianity which was a carbon copy of African universal Spirituality. The first thing the Europeans did was to laugh at the African gods. Then they made the Africans laugh at their own gods. Europeans would go on to colonize the world. They not only colonized the world, they would also colonize information about the world, and that information is still colonized. What they would deal with was a carbon copy of Christianity as interpreted by foreigners. This Christian slave trade hit Africa at a moment of internal weakness and Africa was part of the catastrophe before it could recover its strength.

In the Americas and in the Caribbean Islands we find Bartholomew de las Casas, who came on Christopher Columbus' third voyage and who sanctioned the increase of the slave trade with the pretense that this would save the Indian population. When the Pope sent commissions to inquire into what was happening with the

Indians, many of the islands did not have one Indian left, they were all dead. It was at Christopher Columbus' suggestion that the slave trade was increased to include more of the Africans, again, under the pretense of saving the Indians. It was the same Christopher Columbus who says in his diary, "As man and boy I sailed up and down the Guinea coast for twenty-three years . . . . " What was he doing up and down the coast of West Africa for twenty-three years? The assumption is that he was part of the early Portuguese slave trade. Now is he still your hero? When you look at the Western hero and how he became a hero, when you look at all those people they called, "The Great," and find out what they were great for you will then have a new concept of history. There are a number of good books on this subject. Two of the more readable are by Eric Williams, late Prime Minister of Trinidad, formerly teacher of political science at Howard University. They are *Capitalism and Slavery*, and his last big book, *The Caribbean from Columbus to Castro*.

The subject of this talk is really "The African Inventor in the New World and His Contribution to Technology, Medicine and Science." While I may be going too long way round, I'll get to the subject. But you will have to know what happened behind the curtain of slavery and the consequences of the Africans' enslavement and to what extent Europe recovered from its lethargy and to what extent Europe exploited people outside of Europe. But the main thing that you have to understand is that the African did not come into slavery culturally empty-handed. In order to stay in luxury, Europe had to have large bodies of people to exploit outside of Europe where they could get land and labor cheap. Where they could get control of other people's resources, cheap or for nothing. This is what apartheid is really all about. It is about Western control of the mineral wealth of the African. Africa is the world's richest continent, full of poor people, people who are poor because someone else is managing their resources. Do you think that if Africans had all the gold and manganese and zinc and bauxite and uranium that comes out of Africa they would be going around begging anybody for anything, drought or no drought? Have you ever sailed down the Congo River and seen all the vast bodies of water flowing into the sea? The Nile River sustained the greatest civilization the world has ever known, and it rarely ever rains in the Nile River. Yet this one river sustained civilizations for thousands of years, because Africans, at that time, knew what to do with water, and how to direct it in the way they needed it.

Still going to my subject, my point is that the African was brought to the Western world and survived through his inventiveness, imagination and his spiritual attitude. Without these he would have not survived. The African was hit harder than the so-called Indian. Where one died the other would survive. It is not that one had spiritual attitude and the other did not, they both had spiritual attitude and they both had culture. But many of the Africans had come out of pluralistic cultures and were more accustomed to the nature of change.

Now, let's get on to the African's inventive mind. The preface to all of this is to deal with the free African craftsman in the Western world and how these craftsmen became free, that is, "free" with a question mark! In the Caribbean where Africans were brought in large numbers, once they were taken over by the British and others their condition as an enslaved people was exploited. A class of Englishmen who had earned no considerable respect in England, came to the Islands as mechanics. Because their white face was a premium and because they were given privileges and guns and land and had access to African women, they considered themselves as belonging to the exploitive class. They literally exhausted themselves. But the Englishmen did not have the skills they found were needed on the islands and they began to disappear, physically, due to death from exhaustion or return to England. The African craftsmen began to replace them. We now see the beginnings of the Africans' inventive mind in the Caribbean Islands. The same thing was happening in parts of South America. Many times the English would bring over English-made furniture and there were some termites in the Caribbean. Some of these termites are still there, and when the termites began to eat up the soft wood in the English-made furniture, the African with his meticulous mind began to duplicate that furniture with local hard wood. This was done especially in Jamaica where they had large amounts of mahogany then. Jamaica does not have mahogany now because the mahogany forests were overcut to the point where Jamaica now has no considerable variety of mahogany.

Some of the most beautiful mahogany in the world used to come from Jamaica.

As with the disappearance of the British craftsmen, when the African craftsmen began to emerge, something else began to emerge in the Caribbean Islands. A class of people whose crafts maintained plantations. The Africans saw how important they had become and began to make demands. This is the origin of the Caribbean freeman. These freemen were free enough to communicate with other Africans, free enough to go back to Africa, and free enough to go to the United States. These freemen from the crafts class began to mix friendship with another group of freemen in the United States. Now, how did the freemen become free in the United States? Mostly in the New England states where the winters were so long that it was not economically feasible to support a slave all year round, when they could be used only for four or five months. Slavery would have been just as brutal as it was in the South if the weather permitted. In New England the slaves had become industrial slaves. A large number of them were employed as ship caulkers. In the era of wooden ships, every time a ship came in the caulkers would have to drill something in the holds of the ship to keep it from eroding and to keep it from leaking at sea. A large number of Africans became ship caulkers and a large number became industrial slaves and they began to learn basic industrial skills. Professor Lorenzo Green's book, *The Negro in Colonial New England,* is especially good in explaining the details of this transformation during the period of slavery.

There were also slave inventors, but these slaves could not patent their own inventions. They had to patent them in the name of their masters.

Soon after the latter half of the nineteenth century, when the Africans understood that emancipation was not the reality they had hoped for, they began another resistance movement in the hope of improving their condition. They set up a communication system with all the slaves. There were no "West Indians," no "Black Americans." These were names unknown to us in Africa. We were and we saw ourselves as one people, as African people.

In the nineteenth century the Africans began the inventive period, and before the beginning of the twentieth century Africans had already invented some of the things that made life more comfortable for many in the United States. When you study a list of the numerous inventions of Africans you will find that they would invent things first and foremost to make life better for themselves. Benjamin Banneker was the first notable Black inventor. When the Africans arrived in the United States, in 1619, the year before the Mayflower people arrived, they were not chattel slaves, but indentured slaves. Indentured slaves worked so many years and then they were free. Most of the indentured slaves were whites. Many times whites and Blacks did not see the difference in their lives. They were both exploited, and they both had to work so many years before they were free. Therefore, during this time, there was a period when Africans and whites saw no difference in their plight and this was before prejudice and color differences would set in. Many times they married one another and nobody cared; they were both slaves anyway. Out of these marriages came some people who helped to change the condition of the slaves in the United States. Benjamin Banneker was a product of one of these relationships. In his mother's time if a white woman had a Black lover and because of her whiteness she worked her way out of the indenture ahead of her lover, then she came and bought him out of the indenture and married him. No one took notice.

Benjamin Banneker, literally, made the first clock in the United States. He dabbled in astronomy, he communicated with President Thomas Jefferson and he asked Jefferson to entertain the idea of having a secretary of peace as well as having a secretary of war. He was assistant to the Frenchman L'Enfant who was planning the City of Washington. For some reason L'Enfant got angry with the Washington people, picked up his plans and went back to France. Benjamin Banneker remembered the plans and Benjamin Banneker is responsible for the designing of the City of Washington, one of the few American cities designed with streets wide enough for ten cars to pass at the same time. This was the first of many of the African-American inventors that we have with good records. There will be many to follow and I am only naming a few.

James Forten became one of the first African-Americans to become moderately rich. He made sails and accessories for ships. During the beginning of their winter of the American Revolution it was noticed that the tent cloth they were using for the tents was of better quality than the cloths they had in their britches. James Forten, the sail maker, was approached to use some of the same cloth to make the britches for the soldiers of the American Revolution. These britches, made by this Black man, saved them from that third and last terrible winter of the American Revolution. Now, the role of Blacks in the American Revolution is another lecture in the sense that 5000 Blacks fought against the United States on the side of England in the American Revolution, and the English had to find somewhere for them to go after the war. They sent some of them to Sierra Leone, but some of them went to Nova Scotia.

Jan Ernest Matzeliger, a young man from Guyana, now called Surinam, invented the machine for the mass production of shoes; this invention revolutionized the shoe industry.

In summary, African-Americans continued to create inventions. They revolutionized the American industry. For example, Granville Woods not only revolutionized the electrical concept, but he laid the basis for Westinghouse Electric Company. Elijah McCoy invented a drip coupling for lubrication that revolutionized the whole concept of lubrication. He had over fifty patents to his credit and so many whites stole from Elijah McCoy that anytime a white man took a patent of a lubrication system, or anything that related to it to the patent office, he was asked, "Did you steal it directly from McCoy or did you steal it indirectly from McCoy or is it the real McCoy?" This is how the word came into the English language, "the real McCoy."

In the closing years of the nineteenth century the greatest talent was that of Lewis Latimer. He was not only a draftsman, but he drew up the plans for the telephone. Alexander Graham Bell was the one who invented the telephone, but the patent that had to be drawn up, all the moving parts and all of the vital parts was done by Lewis Latimer, a Black man. Latimer also did a few other things that don't make me too happy. He improved the Maxim gun that became the forerunner of the present day machine gun. He is also responsible for the flourescent light. He wrote the first book on the incandescent light that you know as the flourescent light. He worked with Thomas Edison. He was one of the Thomas Edison pioneers. While Thomas Edison created the principle of the electric light, his light went out in twenty minutes. But the man who created the filament made the light go on indefinitely. That was Lewis Latimer, and he deserves as much credit for the electric light as does Thomas Edison. And he and his accomplishments were completely left out of history. Only Thomas Edison's accomplishments are mentioned.

Not only did African-Americans invent a lot of other things, including labor-saving devices, African-Americans have played a major role in getting America into space. In space medicine the leading doctor is an African-American woman. The person that designed the interior of the ship, including the disposal facility, is an African-American man. When they sent some astronauts up without instructing them in his method of disposal of waste matter, a near catastrophe occurred. The space buggy that they used to walk on the moon was, basically, a Black invention and so is the camera that they used on the trip to the moon.

You might wonder that after all that the African-Americans have contributed in making the United States comfortable, even to the couplings that hold all the weights together when trains are moving around the country, why are they having so much trouble, and why are they still having difficulty? Principally because we were not brought to the United States to be given democracy, to be given Christianity. We were brought to labor and once the labor was done, we were an unwanted population in the United States. We were a nation within a nation searching for a nationality.

When we put all of us together, we are larger, in number, than all of the nations in Scandinavia put together. Their population would not be as large as the African-American population in the United States alone. According to the statistics of the United Nations and the *Jewish Year Book* all the Jews in the world would come to less than one-half the number of African-American population in the United States. Yet Israel gets more financial aid than all of the African nations in the world put together. Principally because we have not developed the political apparatus to put the right pressures on the leaders in the world to make it so.

I see no solution for African peoples, any place in this world, short of Pan-Africanism. Wherever we are on the face of this earth we are an African people. We have got to understand that any problem faced by Africans is the collective problem of all the African people in the world, and not just the problem of the Africans who live in any one part of the world. Once we put all of our skills together, and realize that between the United States, the Caribbean Islands, Brazil and other South American countries there are 150 million African people, and the population of Africa has been counted as 500 million for over fifty years, implying that the African man has been sleeping away from home, and you know that is not true.

In the twenty-first century there are going to be a billion African people on this earth. We have to ask ourselves, "Are we ready for the twenty-first century?" Do we go into the twenty-first century begging and pleading or insisting and demanding? We have to ask and answer that question and we have to decide if we are going to be the rearguard for somebody else's way of life, or do we rebuild our own way of life, or will we be the vanguard to rebuild our own nation.

We have to say to ourselves when we look at our history, the great Nile Valley civilization, the kind of civilizations we built on other rivers, the Niger, the Limpopo, the Zambezi, the kind of civilizations that gave life to the world before the first Europeans wore shoes or had houses that had windows. We need to say to ourselves, with conviction, that, "If I did it once, I will do it again."

QUESTIONS AND ANSWERS

Q I would like to show my appreciation to Dr. Ben and our Senior Professor. I would like to ask this question: I found after some research in Egyptian history quite a bit of confusion regarding the people who passed through Libya to get to Egypt. Are they called the Hyksos, and how do you distinguish between them and the so-called Hebrews?

Dr. ben-Jochannan: The only evidence that we have in any of the hieroglyphics is that the relations of the Hyksos who came there in the Thirteenth Dynasty and destroyed the Thirteenth Dynasty, were themselves kicked out. In the Seventeenth Dynasty the ancients call them an ignoble people. There were no descriptions for them physically or otherwise other than they came from a tributary to the Onynx River. In examining the maps we find that the Onynx is a small tributary coming from the Euphrates. Onynx statues in the museum in Cairo show the Hyksos; other than that there is no positive distinction except at the Temple of Pekorone at Abydos in what is called the Throne Room, the King Room. You have the listing of the Cartouches, but there is no name for them. They once stated that they were a people who had come in to the Delta region and were allowed to live there, but the exact time of the Hyksos seems to be the exact time of the people called Haribu, later called Hebrews and now called Jews, or Semites, Harmites, Jarfites and so on. But this is about the amount of knowledge that we have about the Hyksos that will bring them to the Thirteenth or Fourteenth to the Seventeenth Dynasty.

Q I would like to thank both people for speaking tonight. One theme that runs throughout the discussion has been the colonization of information, not only technology, but information per se. We all realize that the Western media are still biased in the presentation not only of Africa, Mother Africa, but equally of all third world peoples. What do you recommend as some sort of strategy to adopt vis-à-vis this disinformation, especially when institutions like UNESCO can no longer be acceptable given the fact that the United States and Great Britain, who both claim to be very democratic nations, have withdrawn from such a body?

Dr. ben-Jochannan: I did not understand the question as thoroughly as I thought I should have. Repeat the last part of it.

Questioner: In the last part I was saying that countries like Great Britain and the United States have withdrawn from UNESCO, and that was one of the main channels through which information could get through, especially when it came to the recommendation of text books. Now doesn't the panel think that by withdrawing from the body they are somewhat perpetuating the status quo? And if that status quo is perpetuated what will be the strategy to adopt so that this disinformation ceases?

Dr. Clarke: I think that Africans need their own UNESCO. I think that the Organization of African Unity should have a similar information gathering agency with or without the consent of the Arabs. If the Arabs want to go let them go. Anybody who doesn't want to stay in our house and be committed to our house should leave our house. The United States formed UNESCO because they thought it would be a private Western club. And when the Africans wanted to use it, they wanted to pull out. We see the organization of the International Congress of Africanists, when the Africans are beginning to demand a new concept of African history from an African point of view; the organization of the Monument Commission when

Africans have begun to demand the restoration of their own art and monuments and also the return of so much of the art works that had been taken out of Africa, most of it right here in England. In essence, Africans are demanding the decolonization of information about the world and out of this has come the new UNESCO History of Africa, looking at Africa mainly through the eyes of Africans. And as good as it is, it is not as good as it needs to be. But it is an improvement on other concepts, and once you replace yourself with respectful human history you will lose your dependency. The Western world has no vested interest in your losing your dependency. The Africans will be ready to organize their own wealth with enough African minds to have the equivalent of UNESCO within the context of the African world with African scholars.

Q I have a question for Dr. Ben and Dr. Clarke. Dr. Ben, my first introduction to Egyptology as a child was some disease that made African noses flat and lips wide. And Dr. Clarke, I'm a little confused in terms of the slave trade and the position of the Moors. What was their role in Spain and Portugal at the time when the slave trade was instituted? Were there some Africans involved or Arabs involved, or Moslems involved or not?

Dr. Clarke: The Arabs held Spain and Portugal with the help of the Africans, mainly military help. And the Arabs turned against the Africans at their own convenience. We haven't dealt with this, the fact that everybody in history we have ever befriended has turned on us when it was at their convenience to do so, and the fact that we owe no favors in this world. We are non-obligated people.

Dr. ben-Jochannan: As a matter of fact, any greatness of Spain, Portugal and southern France was from 711 to 1485 A.D. The European enslavement had already begun and continued through the invasion of Africa by the French in 1830 at Cueta until the Berlin Conference of 1884 and the Brussels Conference of 1890. What happened in terms of Akhnaten or Amenhotep IV with respect to the El Amarna which is now called the Tell el Amarna art style? When you look at early Ethiopian pictures you will notice that the head would be extremely long, because the interest will just be the head. You will notice that in many African pictures, and they are not fetish (by the way it is not in Feteh). To the European it was normal to call all things from Africa, particularly those statues that are gruesome, fetish. It can't be fetish as it is not from Feteh. Feteh is a place in Ghana, where the Portuguese came and found some statues and they said this is fetish. Yes, it is fetish because it came from Feteh.

The hair style of Amenhotep IV shows the symbolic way of "a dress": the hair, the face and so forth, no less so than when you look at Queen Pariah of the nation of Punt/Puanit, which is now called Somalia, Kenya, Tanganyika and Uganda. Anything of all shapes that we consider to be our beauty has to be less than beauty if it is going to be spoken of by the Europeans. The same thing is said about the Chinese and Japanese, that something was wrong with their eyes because they are slanted. The European eyes are not slanted. Those of you in anthropology will know that this is the most racist subject in the whole system, and yet that is the basis upon which we judge all people, by European standards. And lastly, I laugh very much when I see African women in the United States running for Miss America contest, and I ask them what value are you basing this physical structure on?

Q I would just like you to explain because there is a conference coming on in New York in a couple weeks time. The Third Ancient Egypt Conference, and I know this conference and the series of conferences which are taking place are dedicated towards developing the African world view. And you said that the next conference is in Egypt (I hope everybody here can go to Egypt for this conference), but could you tell us basically what is the basic world view of the Association for the Study of Classical African Civilization? What is the association doing about getting a chapter in London? Because when you come here today you see mostly young people who are Pan-Africanists. And we are the people who are working to make the twenty-first century the century of the African people.

Dr. ben-Jochannan: The Association for the Study of Classical African Civilization (ASCAC) is just a research institute based on the purpose of finding information as requested by African people, producing that information and disseminating it amongst the African community. That's primarily what it is. The unique thing about it is that we do not make European-style degrees a criteria for the academician. For when we look at our academicians we have people such as Hubert A. Harrison, otherwise known as the walking encyclopedia, J. A. Rogers, C. L. R. James, and thousands of others who kept our African culture and heritage going when those of us with our Ph.d.'s. and other things did not give a damn. The association is open and if you didn't get an invitation, I'm sure it's an oversight. It isn't that no one wants you, because the interest is for African people all over the world. We have people coming from the Caribbean. As a matter of fact we have twenty-eight brothers coming from Nigeria for the conference. They came from Nigeria by way of Ohio, because they are at the University of Ohio. But nevertheless they are coming as an African group from the motherland. And anyone who wants to come is free to come. I understand, even at this late date. I'm not in charge of the public relations or anything like that. We are elders, and as elders we don't even have a vote. We are advisory people. We have gone back to the old African system where the elders counsel and are asked for their views without dominating. So I hope I'm speaking for my elder, Professor Clarke, who is saying that you are welcome. He'll find places for you, if you can't afford a hotel. There are five homes. The Egyptian conference is a part of that conference. It is based in that association.

Q I would like to show my appreciation for all that I've heard this evening, and I have two brief questions. The first one concerns the word "Africa." Gerald Massey in the *Book of the Beginnings* talked about the Egyptian origins by the pronunciation "Afru-ika." I would like some clarification on this, please.

Dr. ben-Jochannan: "Afru-ika" comes from the Greek language, "Afrik," and it was the Greek "ae" really and then you had "ika," so you had two Greek words that was compounded in one word to become "Africa." "Afriaeka" was the Greek way of saying "the land to the south" and it was to the south of Greece, so they called it Afriaeka and then it became Africa. So that was what Massey was talking about.

Questioner: What he actually said, if I remember rightly, was that, instead of the word "Africa" which is dedicated to the Greeks the word "Afru-ika" actually has an Egyptian connection.

Dr. ben-Jochannan: It is not a word in the Egyptian language that I know, neither in the hieratic of the demotic language that I'm quite familiar with in my research. Furthermore there is no "o" as such in the hieratic or the demotic. Now Massey, he did no research in Egypt. By the way, his main interest was to prove atheism, not to prove the Egyptians as such. He happened to use Egypt and the African writings to show the concept of God as having no basic historical value in terms of truth and that is what Massey spoke about in the *Book of the Beginnings*. He was only making a joke of the Judaic, Christian and Muslim influence as you know. So Massey was not a historian in Africa; he used African history for the proof of atheism. I think the best person you would use is Professor Jackson, who wrote a number of books. He's just had a reprint of his *Christianity Before Christ* and *Man, God and Civilization* which will help very much in respect of Massey's position.

Questioner: In respect of materials that will help, the second question is: I heard you earlier on using Osiris, but you gave us Heru as the African name. Now, what materials are there to identify the African origins, as opposed to the Greek argument we have today?

Dr. ben-Jochannan: When you read the indigenous works ... let's say you go to the temple and you read the various papyri. You will notice that the papyri are written in the indigenous languages, either in demotic, or hieratic and there are various other scripts which have not yet been decoded. For example, I said to you, Rameses III. In fact there is no such name. It is Rame-as-aris. But the Europeans noticed in their decoding that anytime a classical Greek word repeated itself, it was such that they were able to decode it. But there are no vowel sounds. That is why the vowel sound cannot be spoken. Thus, when the Greeks said "Amenophis," it could be written in any way you wanted depending on your language. However, when you read the Medunetcher, it says Amen-Hotep, instead of Amenophis. Even when you say Amenhotep IV, there is no third, fourth, fifth mentioned anywhere in the writing. They used these numerals to make a distinction between this one and that one and the other. Because they don't want to say, Amen-Hotep, Amen-Ra to avoid having to say all those things. It's used for their own convenience.

 You mentioned in the lectures the name "Jesus Christ."

Dr. ben-Jochannan: In Greek, Joshua Christus means Jesus the Anointed; all that the word "christus" means is "to anoint."

Questioner: And you do mention Ethiopia?

Dr. ben-Jochannan: That was not until the Nicene Conference in 325 A.D. ordered by Constantine, the Roman Emperor, when he appointed the 219 Bishops. Because there was such an argument among the African Bishops who had started the church in Alexandria with Panteus and Boetius. What happened at the Conference was that the Romans and other Europeans could not have a woman at the head of a religion, in the person of the Goddess Isis, which later became the Greek name for Aset. It said "Holy Aset, blessed is the fruit of thy womb, Heru," which became "Holy Mary, Mother of God, blessed is the fruit of thy womb, Jesus." Aset was worshipped before Heru, her son; Mary was worshipped before Jesus.

The European did not set a woman over a man, and thus Constantine ordered 219 bishops to revise the whole thing to make Jesus higher than his mother, who became the mother of God, and changed the Herculean worship of Aset. And it is at that point that Jesus not only became higher than his mother, but became born in Bethlehem instead of a cave in Ethiopia. It is at the conference that they equally took out eighteen books of the Bible, thus giving you a book with eighteen chapters missing. The reason for this is that one of the books called *The Book of Genealogy* speaks of Jesus with the skin of a chimney. In the book of Matthew we read of the Angel of the Lord telling Mary and Joseph to take the little boy into Africa. Of course, the Bible doesn't say Africa, but Egypt. If he said take the little boy to London it would mean England, right? Herod the King was going to kill the little boy, so Herod had his men check every family, and every household for this little, golden-haired boy.

Q The questions that I want to ask Dr. Ben are: How do you see history or your role in our community as a vehicle for bringing about social change? What do you see our history internationally in the context of our situation at present? Dr. Clarke talked specifically about brothers and sisters participating in space programs? What I want to know is, how do you see those achievements in the context of the unity that we must achieve and how do you see it in the context of the unity that we don't have?

Dr. Clarke: First, you have to deal with the disunity and how it came about, and how Europe and America have a vested interest in keeping African people divided all over the world. And to what extent they have had a great deal of success in this device. What you have to understand is that there is no society in the world to make another people permanently comfortable within the context of that society. That, when people built a structure in society they built it to protect themselves. If you are going to have comfort and peace you have to build it for yourself. You will never find a home outside the context of the society and the culture of your own creation. Nobody else is trying to do it but you.

 Referring to Egypt and their technology and science, you know there are some who say that we couldn't have built the pyramids. Often people have said, "You people have not had a Rembrandt or a Michelangelo." I wonder if you will talk about art in relationship to science and technology in Egypt and Africa.

Dr. ben-Jochannan: First of all, I would like the young brother to know that I recognize him physically and by voice. Let me clarify by saying that I'm not only a person in what they call the "soft science." Anytime Europeans do something or didn't do it, and it's of no importance, it came out of space. One time they said Zimbabwe was built by ship-wrecked Greeks, and when they found that the Greeks had not gone down there yet, then it became ship-wrecked Chinese, who were ship-wrecked in the middle of Africa! And so finally Ian Smith made it punishable by six months to say that an African did it. Indeed, should you go to jail for saying that an African built Zimbabwe?

Now that Ian Smith is gone, they now admit that, yes, Africans did it. But when we go to the pyramids we have no doubt about it; we've got a 300,000[-person] workforce. What happens? As a pharaoh or a queen is inaugurated and coronated they immediately start building the final resting place. In the early days they built a pyramid and put the resting place low down into the ground until the Third Dynasty. For example, the pyramid of Zozer is ninety feet deep in the ground; that is African engineering, where tunnels run into each other, ninety feet down. When you go to Sakhara/ Saggara, you see the connection between that of Unas and Zozer; all of them connected with a ninety-foot tunnel. The pyramids of Giza are all made of solid stone. The art form has various dimensions. It depends on what you are looking for. If you are looking in the pyramid, you are talking about the history of the Pharaoh plus his view of the next world; his understanding and his scribes' understanding. Then you talk about the writing on the inside of the wall of the pyramids, the chamber where the dead body would be and the materials relating to that. When you come out of the pyramids and you go into the tombs you have a third form of writing, the death of this Pharaoh as he travels from the gates. Then you come to the *Book of the Dead*, showing all these figures and characterizations. Then you go to the *Book of Judgment* where you meet Goddess Maat, and here the art form changes. They are showing you animals, birds which represent qualities and features of the god that is in that particular place. The art form changes again when you go to the Mastaba. This is the building next to the pyramids, where officials of state were buried, like the prime ministers and so forth, who were given permission by the pharaoh and the queen that they could be buried there. That is now the art of the people. The Mastaba deals with the common lives of the people. Now the art form changes again when you get to the temples, for example, the temples of the God Sobek and the God Osiris. You see the 13-month calendar, twelve months of thirty days each and one month of five days which they still have and the farmers used. You see the medical instruments. There were the roads that were in themselves a form of art.

Rameses II introduced another art form where they dug into the stone, and during the reign of Rameses III the art form changed again. So you see it was not an art form, it was art forms changing as the society progressed and developed. Some of the art forms used colors as symbols. If they showed white, it meant the state of death. When it showed black it meant life. But those colors could vary, not in that chronological order. So you have got to understand the period of time whether it was religious or whether it was secular, war, or whatever.

Dr. Yosef ben-Jochannan

THE NILE VALLEY CIVILIZATION AND THE SPREAD OF AFRICAN CULTURE

W hen we speak of the Nile Valley, of course we are talking about 4,100 miles of civilization, or the beginning of the birth of what is today called civilization. I can go to one case of literature in particular which will identify the Africans as the beginners of the civilization to which I refer. And since I am not foreign to the works of Africans in Egypt, otherwise called Egyptians, I think that should be satisfactory proof. This proof is housed in the London Museum that is holding artifacts on Egypt. In that museum you will find a document called the *Papyrus of Hunefer*. At least you should find it there. It was there when Sir E. A. Wallace Budge used it in his translation as part of the Egyptian *Book of the Dead and the Papyrus of Hunefer*.

It was there at that time, a copy of which is in the library of Syracuse University in New York, and I quote from The hieratic writing, "We came from the beginning of the Nile where God Hapi dwells, at the foothills of The Mountains of the Moon." "We," meaning the Egyptians, as stated, *came from the beginning of the Nile*. Where is "the beginning of the Nile?" The farthest point of the beginning of the Nile is in Uganda; this is the White Nile. Another point is in Ethiopia. The *Blue Nile* and *White Nile* meet in Khartoum; and the other side of Khartoum is the Omdurman Republic of Sudan. From there it flows from the south down north. And there it meets with the Atbara River in Atbara, Sudan. Then it flows completely through Sudan (Ta-Nehisi, Ta-Zeti or Ta-Seti, as it was called), part of that ancient empire which was one time adjacent to the nation called Meroe or Merowe. From that, into the southern part of what the Romans called "Nubia," and parallel on the Nile, part of which the Greeks called "Egypticus"; the English called it "Egypt" and the Jews in their mythology called it "Mizrain" which the current Arabs called Mizr/Mizrair. Thus it ends in the Sea of Sais, also called the Great Sea, today's Mediterranean Sea. When we say this, we want to make certain that Hapi is still God of the Nile, shown as a hermaphrodite having the breasts of a woman and the penis of a man. *God Hapi* is always shown tying two symbols of the "Two Lands," Upper Egypt and Lower Egypt, during Dynastic Periods, or from the beginning of the Dynastic Periods. The *lotus flower* is the symbol of the south, and the *papyrus plant*, the symbol of the north.

But we need to go back beyond Egypt. I used "Egypt" as a starting point, in that of all the ancient civilizations in the world, Egypt has more ancient documents and other artifacts than any other civilization one could speak of. So when you hear them talking about "Sumer" and "Babylon," and all those other places, theoretically, they can't show you the artifacts. Thus my position is, first hand information is the best proof; and I can show you the bones and other remains of Zinjanthropus Boisei about 1.8 million years ago. But no one can show me the bones and remains of Adam and Eve, et al.

So I have the proof and you have the belief. If you want to see it you can go to the Croydon National Museum in Nairobi, Kenya; there, you'll see the bones of Zinjanthropus Boisei. If you want to see the remains of "Lucy," you can go the National Museum associated with the University of Addis Ababa. Of course, there are a host of other human fossils that existed thousands of years ago all over Africa; but you can't find one "*Adam*" or one "*Eve*" in any part of Asia.

But we have to go beyond that. We can look at the artifacts before writing came into being. We will then be in archaeological finds along the Nile. Also you would find that there were two groups of Africans; one called "Hutu," and one called "Twa." The *Twa* and *Hutu* takes us back into at least 400,000 B.C.E. (Before the Common "Christian" Era) in terms of artifacts. The most ancient of these artifacts, one of the most important in Egypt, is called the "Ankh," which the Christians adopted and called the "Crux Ansata" or "Ansata Cross." The *Ankh* was there amongst these people, equally the "Crook" and "Flail." All of these symbols came down to us from the Twa and Hutu. You know the *Twa* by British anthropologists who called them "pygmies." There is no such thing in Africa known as a "pygmy," much less "pygmies." But the people call themselves *Twa* and *Hutu*, so that's what they are.

If we look at the southern tip of Africa, a place called "Monomotapa," before the first Europeans came there with the Portuguese in 1486 C.E./A.D. (Christian Era), a man called Captain Bartholomew Diaz, and subsequently another European and his group came, one called Captain Vasco da Gama, who came there ten years later in 1496; when they came to that part of Africa they met another group of people there as well, which they called "Khaffirs." Now this is a long time before the Boers came there in 1652. When the Boers came those Africans may have gone to the moon on vacation (or holiday, as you would call it), because they said when they came there they "didn't meet any natives" [Africans] so they say. But one thing is certain, that Bartholomew Diaz and Vasco da Gama had already left records showing that when they arrived there at Monomotapa the Khaffirs (Africans), including the small ones (Khoi-Khoi and Khalaharis) (remember I didn't say "Bushmen" or "Hottentots," that's nonsense, the racist names given them by the British and Dutch Boers), were already there.

So with all of these people that were found in this area we could go back at least 35,000 to 40,000 years to another group of people who left their writings and their pictures. Those people are called Grimaldi. The Grimaldi were there in the southern tip of Africa, and travelled up the entire western coast, then came to the northwestern coast of Africa, and crossed into Spain. Not only in Spain, but all the way up to Austria; it was found that the Grimaldi had travelled and left their drawings in caves all along the way. In the Museum of Natural History, New York City, New York, you can see Grimaldi paintings going back to at least 35,000 years ago. I remind you that it is only about 31,000 years before Adam and Eve! It is very important you realize *that*, the next time you talk about Adam and Eve. So we are told that there is an Adam and Eve that started the world, but *that* is a "Jewish world" and I'm talking about before Abraham, the first Jew.

The country that I am talking about now goes back to a period called the Sibellian Period. *Sibellian I* brings us to a period where you will find hieratic writings, the type that no one in modern times has been able to decipher. *Sibellian II* existed about 25,000 years before the birth of Jesus-the-Christ. *Sibellian III* brings us to about 25,000 years before this coming era, and *Sibellian III* would bring us to about 10,000 B.C.E., in which we now have the Stella Calendar that I spoke about, and the pre-dynastic period will be considered from the same, 10,000 to 6,000 B.C.E. There is an immediate pre-dynastic period between 6,000 and 4,100 B.C.E., and that is the point when High Priest Manetho, in about 227 or 226 B.C.E., attempted to present for the Greeks, who had imposed upon him to write a kind of chronological history of the Nile Valley. Europeans, instead of saying what Manetho said in his chronology of the history of the Nile Valley, forget to say it was at the end of the Nile Valley he addressed. For example, the "*First Cataract*," i.e., an obstruction in the Nile River, is at a place called the City of Aswan, when in fact it is the last; the "Sixth Cataract" is in fact Aswan, Upper (or Southern) Egypt.

This is important to understand, because Egypt, which most of us deal with and forget the rest of the Nile Valley, is not at the beginning of the Nile Valley high cultures, but the end. High culture came down the Nile; but if you go on the Nile you will always hear about the "pyramids of Egypt." Yes, they are the "world's largest"; they will blow your mind, so to speak, but they are not the first pyramids of Africa; they are the last. There are thirty-two pyramids in Sudan, none in Ethiopia, and seventy-two in Egypt. What happened is that as the Africans became much more competent in engineering, etc., they increased the size of their pyramids in sophistication; thus at the end of the Nile you could see different forms and the colossal pyramids, the largest being one by Pharaoh Khufu, whom Herodotus called Cheops, and that would be one of the pyramids built in the 4th Dynasty. The first of the pyramids of Egypt being that by *Imhotep*, for his Pharaoh Djoser/Sertor ("Zozer"), the third pharaoh of the Third Dynasty. The architect was the multi-genius, Imhotep, who introduced to mankind the first structure ever built out of stone, and with joints without mortar or any other binding materials.

Now you could understand if I said that the pyramids in Sudan are older than the pyramids in Egypt, and I simultaneously say that Imhotep built the first stone structure known by man, it would seem to be a contradiction. It is not a contradiction, because those in Sudan were built by two methods. There were some pyramids called silt pyramids, and the second method was mud-brick pyramids. Not the type of "bricks made of mud and straw" mentioned in the *Hebrew Holy Torah*, specifically the *Book of Exodus*. That has to be made clear. How did the silt pyramids come about? That type of pyramid came about due to the Inundation Period of the Nile River. This was the period when the Nile River overflowed its banks bringing down the silt from the highlands of Ethiopia and Uganda, and from the Mountain of the Moon, which the people of Kenya called Kilimanjaro.

It is in this perspective that we are talking about Africa as a people. Because, all of that period of time we are talking about, you can go there now and see the artifacts in museums all over Europe and the United States of America. I'm not speaking to you chronologically, because I am using my recall; let us go back to the event that took place; and as I thought about this, something about medicine came to my mind, I remember going to the double *Temple of Haroeris and Sobek*; Haroeris represented by the Cobra Snake and Sobek represented by the Nile Crocodile. In that temple at the rear, you will find drawings of medical instruments going back to the time of Imhotep. That will bring us to about 285 B.C.E. to the construction of the Double Temple which was during Greek rule. Most of the medical instruments you see there are the exact dimensions, the exact styles and shapes still used in medical operating theaters today. You could see all kinds of symbols relating to the use of incense; you could also find the beginnings of the aspect of the calendars (the dating process for the farmers) the same the Coptic farmers still use, the 13-month calendar, twelve months of thirty days each, and one month of five days. The same one the Ethiopian government still uses, officially; that calendar is still a means of telling time to date. When we go to the Temple of the Goddess Het-Heru (Hathor) at a place called *Dendera*, we see the beginnings of what is called the Zodiac. The French stole the original, and in carrying it to France, in hot pursuit by the Arabs of Egypt, they dropped it in the River Nile. Yet a Frenchman said he remembered everything, and he produced a whole new one within two weeks. So if you read *Revelations*, like this false Zodiac, it has nothing to do with St. John, but in fact Bishop Athanasius. This is the same thing. How could the French remember the stolen Egyptian Zodiac so well? It was rectangular, but what they remembered is circular. Thus it is the French who made the Zodiac they placed in the *Temple of Goddess Het-Heru* for tourists these days, and the tourist guides will tell you that is the French one. So!

You can see that even in those early times we were dealing with astronomy, and Europeans have not gone one inch further than those Africans along the Nile. What you have to remember, however, is that the *Papyrus of Hunefer* deals with the Africans who came down the Nile, who were already using this type of thing: and we must wonder since we don't have the day-to-day date, or enough artifacts to put them together to see the transition. Why is it that the Yorubas of West Africa have the same structure of the deity system as the Nile Valley? I don't remember much because the Yorubas in their own folklore speak of having come from the Nile Valley; so you can stop wondering right there, since it is from their earliest teachings in their folklores.

When we go down the Nile and look at the engineering, and our engineering goes not only to the building of the pyramids by Imhotep, this multi-genius, but equally to the time of Senwosret II, with the division of the Nile water; equally to stop the rush of water. That would put us right back to 2,200 Before the Common "Christian" Era (B.C.E.).

The use of navigation and navigational instruments by using the sun and the stars as navigational tools—we have the best record of that going back even before *Pharaoh Necho II*, who saw the navigation of the entire continent and had a map of Africa in almost the common shape it is; and that dates to ca 600 B.C.E. Whereas Herodotus, who came to Egypt in 457 B.C.E., and Erastosthenes, who came there between 274-194 B.C.E., used maps which were rectangular in shape. They reflected the end of Africa being where the Sahara is, the southern end of the Sahara, meaning that they had no concept of Africa from about Ethiopia south to Monomotapa, now called the Republic of South Africa. It is important to note that England played a major role in most of the distortion that we are talking about.

Then we come again to another part that we are talking about, that is, agriculture, before we even come to writing. At the gathering state, when man observes the seed germinating, and out of that came the religious conflict, which other men are to later follow, comes out of one of the most secret symbols of the religiosity of Egypt and other parts of Africa. We are now talking about the dung beetle, and the observation of the African along the Nile with respect to the dung beetle, otherwise called the Scarab. The dung beetle hibernates, does into the manure of a donkey, horse and the cow, only animals with grass manure. And that beetle remains in there for twenty-eight days; you know that particular beetle died in your mind. And when the beetle finally comes out, what better symbol will you have than the resurrection?

The beetle played the same part in the religion of the Egyptians that spread to other parts of Africa, and subsequently into Judaism, Christianity, Islam, and so on. Thus the beetle became the symbol of resurrection. Of course the religion itself had started then. Just imagine you've got to go back 1000 years and see your woman giving birth to a baby. I hope I did not frighten most of you fellows about childbirth; because if you had some experience of seeing a baby being born, you would be less quick to abandon your child. As you are standing there and this baby comes from the woman's organ. You witness this, while the pelvic region is expanding about four or five inches in diameter for the head to pass through, and you are there. You can't perceive that you have anything to do with this

10,000 or 5,000 years ago. Witnessing the birth of that baby sets you thinking. You immediately start to transcend your mind, and you also start to attribute this to something beyond. Thus you start to believe. You start to wonder; why is it here? Where did it come from? And where is it going? Because you are now experiencing birth! But your experience is coming from a woman. Thus you start to pray and the woman becomes your Goddess, your first deity. She becomes Goddess Nut, the goddess of the sky; and you become God Geb, the god of the earth. You suddenly see the sun in all of this and you realize that when the sun came the light came; and when the sun went, the light went; when the moon came you saw a moon in there and you don't see any light because the light is not shining on it. So you see there is a God, at least there is the major attribute of God because you realize when that doesn't happen, the crops and the vegetation don't come.

You also realize that the sun and the moon make the river rise, and the Africans recording these factors created the science of astronomy and astrology. Astrology, having nothing to do with your love life. Astronomy is the chart of the scientific data of the movement of the planet and the sun and so forth, to the movement of each other. Astrology is a physical relationship of astronomy, the water rising at the high tide and that is what the ancients spoke about and the division of the two disciplines.

It was the Greeks like Plato, Aristotle and others who came and learned. In those days the students would come and read for their education. There were no books to take home, there were no publishing houses like now. You had only one book and most of the subjects were taught orally. Certain instructions were given toe to toe, shoulder to shoulder, mouth to ear. I will go no further than that. Some of you here may know how that was done and under what conditions. The English adopted it and called it Freemasonry. Sir Albert Churchward's book, *Signs and Symbols of Primordial Man*, is a cornerstone of Freemasonry. Churchward was a big man in England. Besides being a physician, he was also one of those who made English Freemasonry what it is today. So in another adaptation, the British took twenty-two tablets from Egypt, brought them here and set up what they called "Freemasonry." Of course, the Americans followed suit.

These Africans had moved along the entire continent. You see, we are treating the Egyptians today as if the Egyptians had a barrier that stopped them from going to other parts of Africa. So we say the Egyptians were of a special race, and they had nothing to do with the other Africans. Can you imagine the Thames River at this side stopping the people from the other side from contact with this side, especially when a man standing over there saw a woman here bathing naked; do you think that that river would stop him? Do you think that the Alps stopped a German from going to see an Italian woman? What makes you think that the little river or a little bit of sand would stop a man from seeing a woman naked over there in Africa? I'm using these common symbols so that you can appreciate what I mean. So it isn't because when you go to Egypt you will notice that the ancient Egyptians are shown by the artist as the ancient Nubians or Ethiopians or anybody else, except when you are talking about the conquerors. In most of these museums they purposely bring you the statues of the Greeks, of the Romans, of Persians, the Assyrians, and the Hyksos. They don't bring you any of the Africans. So when they can't help it, and they need to bring you one that you call a typical African like Pharaoh Mentuhotep III, it is important to Egypt that they have to show him. What they did was to make his nose flat, so you can't tell the difference.

Thus once in a while, but when they couldn't do it, what they did say, was: "Well, Negroes came into Egypt in the Eighteenth Dynasty." Now it couldn't be, because the Portuguese hadn't created Negroes until the seventeenth century, C.E., but how come the Negroes created by the Portuguese have a place they called Negroland, which was in fact the Songhai Empire? In the map you could see where Negroland was, and so how do you get the "Negroes and Negroland" way back in the Eighteenth Dynasty? The Eighteenth Dynasty has such figures as Akhenaton, or Amenhotep IV, and his father, whom the Greeks called Amenhotep III; in the West you would call him Amenophis III. The civilization in Africa did not spread only from along the Nile, but it spread into your own writings, documents, and belief system right here in England.

I now go back to the Etruscans, who later became the Romans; the people of Pyrrhus, who later became the Greeks, because Pyrrhus was what later became Greece. But we don't have these

people until they came from the island of the Mediterranean or the
Great Sea. At the time when they left, the Egyptians were the
colonizers of other Africans in Egypt. Setting up the first educational
system for the people of Pyrrhus, where the borders of Libus (now
Libya) and Egypt meet; a little enclave which later became Africa. It
is there that the educational system for the Greeks occurred, and
from there the Africans moved the system to a place called the city
of Elea. It is there that the Greeks would come. This is after they
left the Greek peninsula, go to the Italian peninsula where they
would meet others to come over to Libus, because they couldn't
come the other way as they were going illegally, sneaking out!
Remember, the period of time of which we are speaking, there is no
writing in Greece yet. Until Homer there is no writing in Greece.
No record you could deal with. Whatever they learned, came from
outside, came from Egypt, came from Babylonia. The Babylonian
writings are part of this origin of Greece as well as the writings from
at least 4100 B.C.E., the First Dynastic period, and this is not when
writing started along the Nile. This is the First Dynasty, when Egypt
reorganized herself from under two men. The war between the
north, headed by King Scorpion, and the south headed by King
Narmer, and that will bring us to about 4,100 B.C.E. when Narmer
started United or Dynastic Egypt.

So the pre-dynastic period was the period of the introduction of
religion, of mathematics and science, engineering, law, medicine and
so forth. The period of documentation also started then to some
extent in the First Dynasty. The period of belief in "One God" really
did not start with Akhnaten, that is, when somebody said there must
be only "One God." But the period of absorbing "One God" didn't
start then, because it is that period in 4100 B.C.E., when Narmer,
after defeating Scorpion, the leader of the North, decided that the
deity of the North, *God Amen* (which you say at the end of every
prayer, you are still praying to the African *God Amen*), be put
together with his own deity of the South, *God Ra*. But they didn't
notice that he made "One God" out of the two, *God Amen-Ra*. He
used them in that respect. But the people fell into civil war and there
was division again. From that union, God Amen-Ra became God
Ptah, and the Goddess of Justice became Maat. Justice, shown as a
scale which is the same symbol now used in the United States for

justice, except that there is no justice in the United States, because one scale is up, the other is down, and that is not justice; that is "just this"! Justice is when both scales are on the same level, and so the African in America who asks for justice is being foolish. The symbol says you will never get it; you'll get "just this"!

Before these symbols came the laws on morality and human behavior, the Admonitions to Goddess Maat—Goddess of Justice and Law. There were forty-two Admonitions to Goddess Maat forming the foundation of justice. Then there are the teachings of Amen-em-eope one thousand years before Solomon stole them, some of which he plagiarized word for word, and others he paraphrased, which are now called the Proverbs of Solomon. And yet if we could have stopped there we would have done enough. But it wasn't the last of it, so to speak. Because we came down with jurisprudence, the basis of law attached to the deity which we are teaching now as jurisprudence. And there is a thing in the African jurisprudence that a harborer should not get away from the penalty of the thief.

During the earliest time of the Kingdom of Ethiopia, King Uri, the first King of Ethiopia had spoken about, "justice isn't based upon strength, but on morality of the condition of the event." This now interprets as "the stronger should not mistreat the weaker"; and this is supposed to be something said by Plato, just like the nonsense we hear that "the Greeks had democracy." The Greeks have never had democracy. They never had one in the past and they don't have it now. When they were supposed to have had democracy in Greece no more than five percent of the people had anything you could call democracy. When you look at that, you find it was from this background going back to the time of Amen-em-eope that these fundamental laws came from, you could see why those laws spread from North Africa and into Numidia, which is today called Tunisia.

It is at Numidia then that Augustine's family, continuing the practice of the Manichean religion, carried it into Rome later in the Christian Era. When he left his education in Khart-Haddas or Carthage, it is that same teaching from the Manicheans that Augustine carried into Rome. Ambrose, the greatest Christian scholar in all of Europe, became stunned. But when this twenty-nine-year-old boy arrived and spoke to Ambrose about his education in Carthage,

Ambrose said, "Man, you're heavy." And Augustine took over. It was the same teachings that Guido the Monk, who went to Spain in the time of the Moors, had taught at the University of Salamanca which they had established. And it was the same Manichean concept that made Augustine write against the Stoics. Augustine wrote the fundamental principle that was to govern modern Christianity in its morality, when he presented them with a book called *On Christian Doctrine*. He had previously written the *Holy City of God*. If you want to check Augustine to see if he was an indigenous African read his *Confessions*. There he will tell you who he was.

When Islam came it was supposed to bring something new, but I ask "what did it bring new?" Because Islam was supposed to have started with an African woman by the name Hagar, according to Islamic literature. Hagar was from Egypt, and Abraham was from Asia—the City of Ur in Chaldea. At the time of Abraham's birth a group of African people, called Elamites, were ruling. Before Abraham, the sacred river of India has been named after General Ganges, an African who came from Ethiopia. The River Ganges still carries the name of General Ganges. And I notice in India they haven't given up the symbolic worship of the cow, which represents the Worship of Goddess Het-Heru, Hathor, the "Golden Calf" of the Jews. They also haven't given up the obelisk that still stays there, which the Hindus copied. Again came an Englishman by the name of Sir Geoffrey Higgins, who published a two-volume work in 1836, and in Volume One in particular, he is speaking about all the deities of the past being "black," but said: "I can't accept that they could have come from even Egypt, they must have come from India." He couldn't accept it!

Out of that religion of the Nile Valley came the Religion of Ngail in Kenya from the same river base. And as the situation changed you had the Amazulu going for it, because the Zimbabwe river is still there. The people who were originally there were kicked off their land by the British, and equally by the Germans. When the German Dr. Carl Peters came there, the struggle between the Germans and the English for Tanganyika was going strong; both sides killed off the people around that area who spoke the local Rowzi language. So when you talk about Zimbabwe, don't think about the nation alone. Zimbabwe also means a metropolis of buildings equal in design to the pyramids' cone shape. When the sunlight coming in strikes the altar, the altar shines because of the sunlight. They had a mixture of gold and silver, the exact thing as what happens when you are down at the rock-hewn Temple of Ramesis II, which is on November 22nd, when the sun comes in past the doors. It also happens in February. This shows the commonality of the African culture throughout Africa.

And lastly, just remember that when you see the Ashantis, the Yorubas, and all the other African people, they were not always where they are now. Arab and European slavery made the African migrate from one part of the African world to the other; that is why you can see in Akan culture as written by the African writer Dr. J. B. Danquah, the people with the same hair-cut, and the same beads and jewelry system as Queen Nefertari (the wife of Pharaoh Rameses II in the Nineteenth Dynasty), and Queen Nefertiti (the wife of Pharaoh Akhnaton in the Eighteenth Dynasty). It is too much to speak about it, really.

If you had known this when you were much younger, you too over there, you would have wanted a nation; for you too would have realized that if you have a golden toilet in another man's house (nation) you have got nothing. It is only when you have your own house (nation) that you can demand anything, because you don't even need to demand anything, you do it. It is only when you have your own nation that you can decide the value and the judgment of beauty. If I was ruling England and you came to run for a beauty contest, you would be disqualified even before you came. You're talking about racism; why not? This isn't your country. You cannot run for a beauty contest in a white man's country. You don't see any Europeans winning any beauty contest in China, Japan or India; but the funny thing is that they come and win one in Nigeria. As a matter of fact Miss Trinidad was a white girl. Miss Barbados also a white girl, and Miss Jamaica was a white girl, all of them in a Black country. And this is what I'm saying. You can call it racist, but you know I'm telling the truth.

What I hope I have done is to make you understand the necessity for further research; but more than all, the necessity to talk to your child. When your physician tells you that you are pregnant that's when you start teaching your child. Talk to the child at the time of birth. This is when his and/or her education starts, before he/she gets out of school, and before you and I die.

Dr. John Henrik Clarke

PAN-AFRICANISM AND THE FUTURE OF THE AFRICAN FAMILY

I n approaching this subject, the first thing you need to know is that for thousands of years before the existence of Europe, what we know as Africa was the world. Our greatest contribution to the world was civilization itself and the concept of family structure. We have not talked enough about our life as a people before the European contact and the negative impact of the Europea presence.

I feel a great deal of sadness as this series is coming to a close. I think if we had talked a little more long ago, the great dialogue started between us would have continued, and the catastrophes of our past would not have started. Before I deal with Pan-Africanism and the future of the African family, let's deal with the preface to it. To do this I will deal with the structure and the design of the African family in the culture before there was a need for Pan-Africanism.

First let's deal with the world "pan," because there is a mistaken understanding about this word. "Pan" means all. Pan-African means all African people. It refers to the oneness of all the people of African descent and it infers African world unity. Last evening the sister brought up the difference between the Pan African Congress and the African National Congress and emphasized the integrationist nature of one and the nationalist nature of the other. She was talking about family and the European's interference in our family disputes. The Europeans think they must interfere in our family disputes and yet they dare not let us interfere in theirs. Let's talk about this mistake that the Africans often make. These mistakes got them in trouble then and it gets them in trouble now. There was a time when the Europeans had more difficulty in uniting, family-wise, than the Africans have right now. There was a time when if the Africans wanted to conquer all of Europe all they had to do was take a few sticks and some sand, the Europeans were that weak. We never took advantage of them at their lowest ebb, but they always took advantage of us at ours. When we had a family dispute, they took advantage of the family dispute to spread disunity. It is the spreading of this disunity that made for the need for Pan-Africanism. Their war on a people is first and foremost a war on the most delicate and the most important unit in a people's existence, the family. This has made you restructure the family all over again. Because of the 3,000 years or more that we were under siege, we have been trying to put that family back together again. Once we put that family back together, and it takes hold successfully, we will walk on the stage of world power and be what we once had been and never again be dependent on any people.

Let's deal with their first assault on the structure of the African family. Dr. Ben has already done this, but let's see whether we can appraise the political meaning of what he has said. He has shown you the structure of the society before the first invasion of Africa, the consequence of this invasion and the history of how Africa survived and developed in spite of the invasion. When we look at the African family and African life before the invasions, the most important unit is the family. The family structure, the structure of the village and subsequently the structure of the larger unit, the city. We quite forget that until 1680 B.C. there was nobody in Africa but African people. The Africans were in complete control of themselves. It is hard for you to imagine that with the bombardment of your mind by Western textbooks and the constant study of Western civilization, exclusively, that there was a time when Africans had all that was meaningful that could be called civilization. It is harder for you to imagine that you existed and had functioning societies 3,000 years before the first European had a shoe to wear or lived in a house that had a window. It has been made difficult with the processing and the conditioning of your mind to see this. What kind of structure did you have and why were you so secure and what caused you to lose it? When you lost it the first time, when the family structure was shattered for the first time, it was not shattered by Europeans because Europe was not even functioning at that time—there was no Europe. Europe is a creation and not a continent. As you look at the map it is northern Asia. Some people from a thawed-out ice-box had come to your land, taken you over, processed your mind into thinking he has always been civilized and you have always been waiting for him to bring the light. What happened when you found out that he had no light? In R. R. Palmer's work, *A History of One Modern World*, he writes of 3,000 to 5,000 years of civilization that had passed before anyone knew that anything like Europeans existed. It is hard for you to imagine that there was a time when not only did Europeans not exist, there was a time when the word did not exist.

Let's now look at what went wrong with the flow of information. How did we get so far off course? Every Scandinavian boy, or any European, or any reasonable thinking white person can claim Greece as his heritage, as his intellectual heritage, although their nations did not exist when Greece existed. At the height of the existence of Greece there was not a single nation-state in the rest of what you now call Europe, so how could Greece be their heritage? Europe, in general, had nothing at all to do with the development of Greece. If you look at the map you see that Greece was one of the nations that was closest to Africa. This proximity put them closest to the intellectual mainstream of the Mediterranean. When the intellectual miracle of Egypt existed (and it existed thousands of years before anybody knew that there was a Europe), it exited based on the feuding of the peoples from the lower end of the Nile River with the upper end of the Nile after the Sahara dried up and there were great cities in this area. The people from the upper end of the Nile gravitated toward the lower end of the Nile and what became Egypt became the reciprocant of the greatest body of power ever assembled in the history of the world. It had already created the greatest and most enduring civilization in the history of the world before anybody had invaded them. The first invaders came from western Asia, now called the Middle East. I guess you are now in the best place to use the word "Middle East," inasmuch as the word was invented here in England.

Why would these people invade in the first place? What were they looking for and what did they do? In the first place they could be classified as thugs of that day and they could be called thugs of this day. They knew nothing about the culture and yet they had filtered into the Africa of that day. They were in the valley of the Nile for one hundred years before the invasion and we have to deal with another kind of invasion which is embarrassing, the sex invasion. When they came a hundred years before, they married into African families and they created a generation of confused bastards with mixed feelings of loyalty. These confused bastards generally showed them how to come into the country and how to conquer their adopted country. The disunity, therefore, began with the destruction and the disruption of the African family structure. Except for this occurrence you will not need this lecture on Pan-Africanism at all.

Now I am about to start my lecture. In the closing years of the nineteenth century when African people all over the world had fought against slavery and its aftermath, and when the Caribbean people understood that their emancipation was a fake and when the African-Americans understood it even better, because theirs was an even bigger fake, the slaves had nowhere to go. They ended up working on the same plantations for a pittance, having to take care of their own families in their own shacks and the European got the best of this situation. The slaves had no place to sell their labor except the same place that they were "liberated" from. And systematically, for economic reasons, a form of re-enslavement started. By the end of the nineteenth century the former slaves began to understand what had happened to them and from the Caribbean the concept of Pan-Africanism was born. It readily caught on among the African-Americans.

In Africa there were African Pan-Africanists, mostly in Ghana and in Nigeria. In Nigeria, there was Majola Adjebebe, the great Pan-Africanist African minister. In Ghana there was Caseley-Hayford, father of modern Ghanaian politics long before the birth of Nkrumah. I assume that in an audience of African people that everyone knows about Joseph B. Danquah. He was, literally, the intellectual father of modern Ghana and the schoolmaster of Kwame Nkrumah. The mantle of political leadership should have passed to Danquah. It was snatched away from him and hurt him terribly.

I assume also that you know of the great minds that came out of Nigeria at the end of the nineteenth century. There were many great lawyers who came to the fore then. In Ghana Casely-Hayford had made communication with African-Americans and with African-Caribbeans, thereby creating a three-way intellectual bridge, and this was Pan-Africanism's beginning.

While Pan-Africanism is still a conversation piece, let's also look at other "pan" movements in the world that did not have anything to do with the African. These movements have been successful no matter how you look at them. No matter how cruel it sounds, the movement of Adolph Hitler was a "Pan" movement, it was a Pan-Germanic movement. What you call the Holocaust was a family dispute between European and European. European racism had split itself outside of Europe. Now the racism that had wrecked the rest of the world turned on itself and wrecked its own people. That is what the essence of the so-called Holocaust was about. I am not saying anything was right about it, and I am not arguing against the six million people that lost their lives. It was wrong. But it was European against European, and they are still not making Europeans pay for it. Somebody outside of Europe will pay for it because the crimes committed against Europeans are nearly always paid for by non-Europeans. The genius of the Europeans is that they have a talent for draining diseases. They have always drained their political sores on the lands of other people. They have the talent for recovering their internal losses by external extraction from people who had nothing to do with the crimes committed against them. This is the basis of the disunity and the destruction of the African family unit in Africa. They did, to some extent, the same thing in Asia.

The thugs from western Asia with their original idea of family structure destroyed, with their society in disunity, with no knowledge of African family structure, began to plan an assault on the African family structure. They did not understand the Africans' basis for culture, they did not understand their religion, and they came like most invaders came to Africa, laughing at their gods. When a people laugh at your gods, they have you one way, and when they train you to laugh at your own gods, they have got you another way. I have said, repeatedly, that not only Africa is in need of a cultural revolution but there will never be a true cultural revolution until an African head of state prays to an African god in public, without apologizing for it. I was and still am a great admirer of Julius Nyerere, but after he started kissing the Pope's ring, I began to question how one who condemns white people in the morning can worship them in the evening, without seeing this as a contradiction of what he stands for.

When World War II ended, a body of African people, mostly African-Americans, were available to Africa and they could have been picked up very cheaply if Africa was organized to do so. Africa would have had a fine modern army. Our enemy had trained us to protect him, and they had taught us the technique of this protection. He had taught us how to kill them when he wanted other Europeans killed, and we did it well. If we had to fly airplanes, we flew them well. We were given guns, and we shot them well. As a result, after the war ended, the largest and best organized African people who knew about modern operational and technical warfare were African-Americans, and they had no jobs that suited these talents. Their skills eroded and the others, a new breed of African-Americans emerged, whose minds were so warped they would kill on command, even if it was their own mother, because of this brainwashing. When I talk about the army Africa could have had, I am talking about Pan-Africanism. Yet the most Pan-African thing he could have done was to organize these people with their technical training to protect Africa. For example, when the raid came at Entebbe in Africa, there was no mass protest. As an African people being truly Pan-Africanist we have to have a military force that would protect African people, anyplace in the world. To do this we have to stop dividing ourselves based on islands and based on color graduation or how close we are to our white fathers.

Liberation is hard. You have to get a little rough to liberate a people. Our mistake that broke up the great unity we had is when we permitted strangers to come into our house who held no loyalty to our house. All people ask you when you come into their house, "What is your loyalty, what is your commitment to this house?" If you have no commitment to the protection of this house then you have to get out of this house. When we permit other people to live among us and to live among us for hundreds of years without any loyalty to us, we are forgetting to practice what I call the "essential selfishness of survival," by failing to check out the loyalty of the stranger. When you find the strongest thing about a people, and identify what is strongest about these people, look closer, because what is weakest about a people is going to show; it is the other side of the coin. One of the strongest things about African people is their humanity, manifested in their ability to accept other people. One of the weakest things about African people is not knowing how to make political use of their humanity for their own protection. This weakness permitted the first invasion of Africa and these constant encroachments on the African culture was a war on the culture and a war on the family that resulted in a breaking up of their family structure.

The consistent invasions which were not dealt with brought about a confusion about definition, about who we were and who we had to relate to. Had we dealt with these first invaders well we would not have the troubles that we are having now. We need to study other peoples' dealing with invaders. Study the invaders of Russia and the invaders of China. The invader very rarely goes home. One third of the Japanese army that invaded China never went home. They just moved around China until they got tired. We have not developed a technique for dealing with invaders, and these invaders have altered the structure of our families that were well-designed and functioned well for thousands of years. This failure made Pan-Africanism necessary, but when we conceived Pan-Africanism we erected it without any kind of protection.

The massive slave revolts in the West Indies and the revolts in Africa were effective, but early in the nineteenth century we produced a nation of talkers who thought they could appeal to the Christian consciousness of the European. That was another mistake. Freedom is something you take with your own hands. It was an illusion for us to think it was going to be delivered to us. It is not something that is left in a will, and one generation could leave it for another generation. Each generation when it gets it must secure its freedom all over again, with their own hands. As a people, this is where we failed: to secure the ship of such freedom as we have. We have to secure it for those now living and not depend on those past.

Another mistake in retrospect: In 1919, W. E. B. DuBois called a conference in Paris and in Brussels. This is a mistake for us as Africans. We are always calling conferences to talk about liberation on somebody else's soil and using somebody else's language to do it. When you look at the Haitian revolution, the greatest difficulty they had after the liberation was that Toussaint wanted to make peace with France and he willingly paid a price too high for it. Allegedly he went to France to negotiate with Napoleon, and was imprisoned because he went alone. When Christophe went to confront LeClerc, he did not go without protection: he was street-wise. He took 3,000 men, surrounded the castle, and faced LeClerc with a band of 50 men. He was not sent to the dungeons because he had protection all around him. He gave an order to the servant of LeClerc. He gave this order to a servant of LeClerc's household who was put there as a spy, and he gave this order in an African language. He was successful, the French then retreated to the hills where the Africans were waiting for them; and all they needed was sticks and stones. This was a military aspect of Pan-Africanism that we have not used, but ultimately will have to use. We will then have to address ourselves to a situation like South Africa and we will have to understand that this is a problem and a struggle for every African who walks the face of the earth. This is something that we cannot leave to the Africans who live in South Africa to handle alone.

Once we understand the nature of Pan-Africanism we should begin to pull these forces together for a concerted struggle for African people all over the world. We will put back together the best unit, the most essential unit in our culture, that is, the African family unit. We will restore the African man as the symbol of authority with that family unit. When you read *The Cultural Unity of Black Africa,*

Diop calls attention to the fact that the African woman had enjoyed liberation far ahead of the European woman. That respect for womanhood was built into the culture and the people adhered to the rules governing this respect. The African woman did not have to fight for liberation, unlike the European woman who was basically subservient and had to be. The African man did not go to war locking his woman in chastity belts.

In the Caribbean Islands, particularly in Trinidad, an island that had not been very active in the three-way intellectual bridge, emerged a man named Sylvester Williams. He founded a group called the Pan-African League and he began to preach the concept of pulling the whole African world together. Here in London he called the first Pan-African Congress, in 1900. DuBois was invited, but the Africans, living in the richest continent in the world, were not invited because they were so poor and could not ask for delegations from Africa. This congress was the beginning of a structural, ideological concept of Pan-Africanism. At this congress they did not ask for freedom. They asked for a means of preparing African people to enter the modern world. They asked, principally, for an improvement in the educational system, an improvement in the quality of education that would prepare the African for living in the modern world: literally, to function in somebody else's world, by somebody else's design, and to function according to the rules laid down by the colonialists. The colonialists, to some extent, were a little sympathetic and a little suspicious.

After the first Pan-African Congress in 1906, many of the great intellectual giants of the African world were still alive—Casely Hayford, John Mensah-Sarbah, the great Ghanaian lawyer, and Herbert McCaulay, the Nigerian, [who] was still young. In the United States W. E. B. DuBois and Booker T. Washington were still alive, and these men began to communicate with one another. Caribbean figures had been coming to the United States since the 1700s and they played a major role in structuring the early African-American freedom movements and the early African-American abolitionist movement. Nobody called themselves "West Indians" or "Negroes" in those days. They were all African peoples, functioning together. Long before they used the word Pan-Africanism they were practicing it among themselves.

What I am talking about is a neglected case in our history, a period when the people from the Caribbean participated in the African-American struggle as part of the world struggle of African people. That concept and the practice of Pan-Africanism, and the unification of the family, started fifty years before the word "Pan-Africanism" came into being; yet something started to go wrong with Pan-Africanism once we attached a word to it. After 1900 conditions in the Caribbean made it feasible for Caribbeans to carry on the concept. Early in the century the concept of union began to give way to some catering to whites that would later harm us. We had thought we would make a few concessions here and there but these concessions still hang like bricks around our necks.

In the African world the nineteenth century was a century of physical confrontation, assaults on our women, assaults on our family structure and assaults on the men of African descent. It is my hope that you will do the job of putting our people together again. The Pan-African concept was a conversational piece up until the end of World War I. After World War I an arrogant dreamer came to the United States after having spent some time here in London. He had learned a great deal in London, but the main thing about the remarkable career of Marcus Garvey is that he never took ideas from a second-rater. He read the ideas of first-rate people. He read the proceedings of the congress held here in 1911. He read those proceedings and his concept of race was grounded. He investigated other people's talks. He was the father of twentieth century Pan-Africanism.

Marcus Garvey was a failure in Jamaica. When he came to the United States he pushed W. E. B. DuBois from the center stage of leadership. When he came to the United States preaching a new concept of Pan-Africanism and African world unity, we needed him more than the people of his native Jamaica and more than any African people on the face of the earth because he reawakened in us certain dreams of unity at a time when the American promise had not been kept. When America had let us know that the American dream was not a dream for us, he said:

In many ways,
In many times,

I will lead you to a new land
A new dream,
And a new promise.

This is why this man's Pan-Africanism had more effect than anybody else's Pan-Africanism. He had attached to his concept of Pan-Africanism the possibility of the establishment of a commercial arm, a military arm and a cultural arm to achieve the liberation and maintain the liberation of African people wherever they happen to be on the face of the earth.

QUESTIONS AND ANSWERS

 From what I understand the British Museum is one of the largest repositories of African treasures in the world, and since we are here what should we be looking for? What would you advise us to check out at the museum?

Dr. Clarke: Well, check out everything. Check out the treasures that were taken out of Egypt. Check out the interpretation of those treasures from that point of view, because you are going to reinterpret them from an African point of view. I think the famous statues are the Ptolemies and they are in the British Museum. I spend days there without fully seeing all of it. The museums of the world are full of stolen properties, mostly stolen from Africa.

Dr. ben-Jochannan: I think there are two museums, particularly in England, among many others you need to look at. Not only the Museum of Natural History, but you need to look at the Egyptian Museum, located a few blocks from each other. Right now there are arguments going on between England and Egypt about "the beard of Khafra" from a statue which the Greeks called Sphinx of Giza. By the way there is no "sphinx" in any part of Egypt. The Greeks had a little female statue which they called The Sphinx; the Sphinx represents a female name. The statue at Giza is of Pharaoh Khafra (who built the second largest pyramid in Egypt; his father, Pharaoh Khufu, built the largest) which you yourself have seen. It is of his head and a lion's body. But the British have refused to return the beard, trying to shake down Egypt for something else they want in exchange for the beard.

You need to look at everything. Not what is exhibited alone, but in the basements. You ought also to look at the second basement for the statue of Socrates and look a second time to see what it looks like. There was one, once in 1938 on the top floor, and it disappeared down to the sub-cellar. When you see it, you will see for what reason. The *Book of Genealogy* will help. You ought to look at the Benin Gates where the British came and shot down the Nigerian professors. In New York at Eighty-First Street and Eighth Avenue in the American Museum of Natural History look at the kind of metal work of the high culture of the people of West Africa.

And so when other people tell you that "your people are not civilized," you need to look here, because it was in the British Museum that a man by the name of Sir Ernest A. Wallis Budge translated the book that he called *The Egyptian Book of the Dead and Papyrus of Ani*, and see that it pre-dated the King James Bible by more than four thousand years. You will also see what the Ten Commandments came out of in a section called the *Osirian Drama*. You will need to look at the *Book of Gates*, also translated here in London. See it right here, either in the basement or on a floor above for display. So you need to look at the museum for civilization. Just as Dr. Clarke said, "You will have to do the same thing in Austria, Moscow, New York, Washington, Italy, Greece, at random to find Africa." Isn't that strange? You need to look at the entire "West" to find Africa, because the "Western people" didn't come to bring us anything. They came in to take away everything, including us.

 I want to know where we can find and more so to liberate our African treasures, not only in Britain, but also in Europe. And when I speak of Europe I am also speaking of the United States of America. I have here in my hand a piece of document which states the Egyptian and Sudanese governments usually allow divisions of the finds made in excavations, not only to the Egyptian exploratory societies here in Europe, but also of other European countries. I would like to ask my two brothers, do they think this is right and how can we get the Egyptian and Sudanese governments to put a stop to this plundering of our great works of art?

Dr. Clarke: As Egyptologists we have been fighting this for a number of years, but let us give an answer as to why. The governments of Egypt and Sudan are not run by Africans. And when the governments of Egypt and Sudan were run by people whose mothers were Africans, namely, Nasser in Egypt whose mother was a Sudanese, or otherwise called Nubian, the same for Sadat, their fathers were Arabs and in Islam your father supersedes your mother in your line of attachment. The Arabs don't give a damn about the treasures in Egypt or Sudan, for in the first place they too like Christians call it "pagan," "heathen," and so forth. The only reason they have it is to bring money to the treasury in tourism. so when we fought them at that point they do give. If you came from Oshkosh and you find two of anything you get one. This is your payment as if they haven't taken enough. And this is only when Egypt got "independence" under Arab control. So there is no interest by the two governments. They don't see themselves as Africans. They consider themselves as part of the Arab world. Only one head of state in Northern Africa considered himself an African and that was Ben Bella who was joining Nkrumah and reminding them (i.e., Arabs) that they have been in Africa for 1300 years and were still acting like Europeans.

You see, either we deal with reality and face the issues or we don't. And a lot of brothers have taken on Islam emotionally to try to defend the Arab cause equally. I don't mind if you take on Islam. You can take on any religion you want. But don't mix Islam and Arabia and or an Arab and Islam. You've got to deal with the Arab position as he or she stands. And so my sister there is no interest by the Arab League, which they still call themselves, and the OAU is subordinate to them. And it is only when an issue is of concern to the Arab League, that they then ask the OAU to back their position. But when the issue becomes downright African, they don't do anything about it. And I say to you and the brothers, go and see for yourselves. Go to Southern Egypt, now called Egyptian Nubia, see what they've done to forty-nine Nubian villages, because of the new dam and the Lake Nasser. Look at the Head of State of Sudan today. Just look at the picture and see for yourself. Yet he can't see Sudan, because he can see Islam before he can see Sudan, and this is the sadness. We see Christianity before we see Africa. We see Judaism before we see Africa. We see all of these foreign things which based all their foundations on Africa, coming back to Africa, and we forget the history.

I think before you can claim anything you must first question the mentality that created that awe. Once you claim the mentality that created the awe you can take it away from those who stole it.

Q 1251 A.D. seems to be the year of effective breaking of power of the African-Arab rule in Spain. Can you tell us the motivation for the actual beginning of the slave trade in West Africa? Can you tell us whether that response to the African-Arab presence in Spain and Portugal was a response to terms of a revenge or was it motivated by factors of trade or starvation as he pointed out?

Dr. Clarke: You answered the top of the question. Let's take the bottom question which is that Africans with every religion they take on are puritans. They out-Pope the Pope, and Abraham and Mohammed. The real arguments that weakened the African-Arab hold on Spain are arguments between the African's and the Arab's interpretation of their faith. And this began with the second Arab invasion. The first Arab invasion was a religious fervor. The Arabs were sweeping across North Africa. Some of them got into Spain and the argument started over what now might be considered by some people to be a minor issue over the treatment of women. Men were marrying more than the customary four and women were staying in the Catholic Church. The African being a puritan resented this. The other thing was that the Arab suffered an identity problem, and when Europe made him an offer he turned on the African in favor of the European. The African especially in North Africa began to swing toward the West, with Mansur and the destruction of the Sudan. The Western Sudan, Songhai, got assistance from the West, and I have a letter between Mansur and Queen Elizabeth of England saying that "if you help me dethrone Antonio of Spain I will give you ammunition to destroy the blacks in Western Sudan."

Dr. ben-Jochannan: The first part of what you stated was again the letter of Bartholomew de las Casas to Pope Julius II. The first group of Africans to go to an island of the Caribbean, Hispaniola, now called "Haiti and Santo Domingo," didn't come straight from Africa. They came from Spain. It was when they started to get rid of the Africans in Spain, after the Moors had lost power, that the first 4,000 were shipped to the Caribbean as slaves. The Spaniards started raiding the coast of North and Northwest Africa. So yes, the Roman Catholic Church was still participating through the Knights of Malta and Knights of Genoa that the Pope placed in charge of the slave trade, and were the ones who were in charge of eliminating the Africans from Spain. That's why you see very few Africans left there at all today. The Spaniards took them first as revenge for 774 years of Moorish/African domination of Spain and the rest of the Iberian Peninsula.

Dr. Clarke: Now what you have to understand in a broad sense is that we have been a people who through history, our friends have never returned our friendship, and everybody we befriended in history has turned on us when it was in their convenience to do so. It came to the convenience of the Arabs to turn on us and to literally sell us and we were the military force that kept them in Spain, and they turned on us. Now there was another party in Spain, who were not only protected by the Africans and the Arabs when the Africans lost their power. They were the Grandees, the money managers of Spain, and they had no difficulty in becoming the money managers of the slave trade. I will leave it to you to guess who they were.

 Could you say something about the Jews financing the slave trade?

Dr. ben-Jochannan: There are Cochin Jews from India, Yemenite Jews from Yemen, Puerto Rican Jews from Puerto Rico, Ethiopian Jews from Ethiopia, and we, all of us, look different. And those from Spain, I didn't call, were all European. So yes, the reason that you have the names Abraham, Solaire, DeSola, and other such sounding names in the Caribbean Islands, and people like me, obviously came from the Jewish slave holders. Nobody wants to deal with the fact that Jews were equally slave holders as well as Christians and Moslem Arabs. Even in the Bible, "Jews are slave holders." And when I asked my mother this question, she says, "This is something we don't speak too much about." But in the Book of Exodus one of the Ordinances says that when you buy a Hebrew slave you must bring him to the doorpost and bore a hole through his ear with an awl; but when you buy a non-Hebrew, in other words a stranger, you must not. The same ministry of priests and rabbis that tells you who owned slaves also doesn't tell you that "the Jews owned slaves" too!

Dr. Clarke: When Mussolini was exterminating African (Ethiopian or "Black") Jews from October 3rd to that morning of October 5th, 1935; that morning when he dropped the bomb on us in the Wal-Wal District, not a single "Western Jew" responded. Professor Tammarat Emmanual of Ethiopia's Hebrew Community even went to the United States to beg aid from the Jews in America. They gave him a mere $400, put him in a boat that had to come through the Suez Canal, in the Mediterranean, and then crossed the Atlantic Ocean. Four hundred dollars, but they didn't know that 1938 C.E. was coming. It was now 1938, and then the European Jews started crying. Mussolini had already exterminated 4.5 million Jews in Ethiopia. We were 5 million when he came; he left us with 500 thousand, and the world said nothing about it. So yes, it doesn't stop me from dealing with the fact that European Jews in Spain participated fully as Grandees (money changers), and as traders. They traded in Isabella's jewelry and things like that to get some money because the Spanish Crown was broke, and they needed the money for the slave trade!

That's history. You don't need Minister Farrakhan of the "Black Muslims" to invent that, nor the Reverend Jesse Jackson. You can't deny that European Jews were, and are, part of European colonialism and imperialism. Where we made the mistake is to separate the two! European Jews are Europeans. When Europeans move because I move in the neighborhood, whether they are Atheists, or Christians or Buddhists, Jews also move. They don't move because they are *Jewish*, they move because they are *white*. They are Europeans, and that is a thing that we must understand; they have played a good game.

Q This question is in two parts and directed at both of you. Firstly, would you agree with the Black Panther view that a people is always subject to slavery. Secondly, after we have freed ourselves mentally, after re-educating ourselves on our historical lands and so forth, why should we still meet with the obstacles which prevent us from obtaining that desire of emancipation, and equality and justice that we really see here on earth? Would you agree with this violent struggle, and would you say to us that it's necessary to use this to attain what we desire?

Dr. Clarke: You have answered your own question because no people ever freed themselves, no people deprived from nationhood ever regained that nationhood without a fight. Non-violence was a strategy that Martin Luther King used and it's a strategy that began to be used. Non-violence was not a way of life, but it was an alternative waiting in the wings. The Hebrews have used violence, historically and at present. Now as for the Panthers, the statement in the verdict of the Panthers was given to them by misguided white liberals who stood aside. They did nothing when the Panthers were being killed by white colleagues, and this deals once more with our concept of alliances. Alliances only use us and walk away from us when we really need them.

Dr. ben-Jochannan: Having heard my elder speak, I was in two wars, one in which the President of the United States of America sent me a letter. I was at the time in Puerto Rico. It said: "Your country needs you." I didn't know until that time that I had a country. This, and the treatment I was receiving! I was in the university then; I went up with two bars on my shoulder, being a Black captain; I couldn't tell a white private to salute me. That changed radically, but still? The second one, I volunteered! This was the one where the Afro-Sharazi in Zanzibar was fighting the Arabs for independence. War is not the best way, it is the time when you may have to kill your own mother, depending on the side she takes.

I think if I had to be asked: "Would you kill your mother in war?," I would say reluctantly, "depending on her position." If a mother takes a position against her children, for our death she may have to die; and there is nobody I like more than my mother. So I say: "a bedbug doesn't appreciate being squeezed to death; it will fight back." I'm not here to tell you when and where, or how, in public; I will not. Dr. Clarke told you that we support struggle, but we will not say against who, when or what, because the most quiet time in your life is when you are sleeping. It is when a group of people decide to attack, because nobody talks, and that's why I know the war in South Africa hasn't started. The youngsters are fighting, but the war in South Africa hasn't started. The war is going to start when the African woman gets tired of hearing that her little teenage boy or girl went to school and came back home in a carton or coffin. She will do what she's done before. Yes, I'm warning Botha. I remember when an African woman would put poison in milk, got special disease for the enemy and committed suicide rather than touch them. It's going to come. That's why I never organize Black women. What I'll do is get a son, organize him and get him with a box of dynamite in his hands and carry him to fight. If you want to see a tank, airplane, and submarine all in one just tell her who did it.

Q As someone concerned about young Black people of this country, I would like to ask your opinion. After seeing what the education system in this country has done to Black people and the tragic things that have happened to them by this system not really teaching them about themselves, about us, and about our past lives, what would you suggest at this moment to be done to rectify some of the damages that have been done to them in the past couple of years? And to prevent them from going to prison, and to be able to know where they are going in their own lives, we would like to know how to tackle this situation?

Dr. ben-Jochannan: They say a man who giveth advice should be able to deal with it. I attack it in my house. I teach my little girls and boys; and by the way, I don't just lecture. I have twelve biological children, nine girls and three boys with three African women.

Two died, and I have had the third one for thirty-eight years. But to talk to a little boy like you talk to a little girl ... well! You see, what happens is that mothers are not talking to their sons, and teaching their son respect for his woman. You see, if I respect my Mama, I'll respect Black women, and that's the reason I am the way I am in the mirror test. I literally give them, when they reach the age of consent, I give them a mirror, a piece of paper and a pencil. I say, write what you see in the mirror. Then I say, look at your Mama and look at your Daddy, and write what you see there. Draw a picture of us, all of us; you, your Mama, and me. Then I make a critique of the picture, or whatever else the writing is. First, the appreciation of self and family, and the racial group; then I make my child an exam for every week. When he (or she) has a school exam every week, he also has mine as an extra on Saturday: twenty questions, and he wouldn't eat until he's finished. I never worry about my daughter, when she is fifteen or sixteen years old, I don't worry. She is trained, brainwashed, programmed. So when I go to sleep with her mother, I don't worry, because I have prepared her for everything including boyfriends. She knows how to handle boyfriends. I prepare both my sons and my daughters, and I think the first step is that brothers must appreciate sisters. A man said, "Tell me how you treat your woman and I will tell you the condition of your race."

Dr. Clarke: I think there is one thing you always have to remember in any educational system, and it is that powerful people never train you how to take that power away from them, and that your oppressor cannot afford the luxury of educating you and asking you to become his oppressor. You will become his master if you were properly educated. If everything that has been stolen from us was given back to us we will not be people begging and pleading. We'll be a people insisting and demanding and we will walk into the chambers of the world and make our demands, and we will be heard, because the art of power is the ability to withhold and to withdraw, and so long as you can make those kind of decisions you have the power, and the major decision that we have to make is whether we are going to continue to be the rearguard for someone else's own, and to remember that no one people ever fashioned a society for anyone other than themselves. If you want a society where you will be permanently comfortable you are going to have to make it yourself.

Dr. ben-Jochannan: I think that it was Frederick Douglass in 1856 or 1858 who was asked the question about why he refused to speak on July 4 (American Independence Day). "What does a Negro have to celebrate on the 4th of July?" He said, "There are those who love freedom and yet deprecate agitation, they want the ocean without the awful roar of its waters," etc. Another man from Jamaica, West Indies, Claude McKay, while in the USA during 1919, answered Douglass by saying:

IF WE MUST DIE

If we must die let us not be like hogs
Hunted and penned in an inglorious spot,
While round us bark the mad and the hungry dogs,
Making their mock at our accursed lot.
If we must die, Oh let us nobly die,
So that our precious blood may not be shed
in vain; then even the monsters we defy
Shall be constrained to honor us though dead!

Oh, kinsmen! (all of you), we must meet the common foe!
Though far outnumbered let us show us brave
And for their thousand blows deal one death-blow!
What though before us lies the open grave?
Like men we'll face the murderous cowardly pack,
Pressed to the wall, dying, but fighting back!

Q We have been reminded once more of our task, let's say for reeducation and informing our people, to reeducate them back to the road of sovereignty. You have been doing marvelously for the adult population, for those who would like to accept and would not reject the truth. My question to you is, what about our Black children, those who we have to depend on to continue on the road to victory? Now a lot of us do have the information that you have there. I would love to see it simplified in some way for our young Black folks. The last thing Dr. Ben said was to construct something for teenagers, but we have a stipulation as we know, to get them when they are young, say, by seven. We have a situation right now watching us in our faces in the United Kingdom with so many Black children denying even the color of their skin. What are you doing to put that information to them?

Dr. ben-Jochannan: I answer this, because as I said I'm used to that condition. I have forty-seven grandsons and seven granddaughters, so you know that I have got that condition. There is such a thing in America called Head Start programs. Kids from three years old to five years old go there before going to the regular kindergartens. I go to one of these every month. I get on the floor, not with this three-piece camouflage suit. I sit on the floor with little children, three to five years old, speaking to them about history, their past, about their parents. Professor Clarke was active in a thing called Haryou-Act. It eliminated no age group of African people.

There are other people in the United States who translate work such as ours into the language of youngsters of elementary and pre-elementary school grades. There are many other writers who are doing that, such as Dr. Barbara Jackson and Beryl Banfield. There are a number of other children's books in the United States showing African heroes, Caribbean heroes, and so forth, and along with these there are a number of independent African schools, some of which are dying because of lack of funds. Some of us don't want anybody to know that we are in a struggle, and that has never stopped.

The African free schools are not something of today, they have always been there except that those of us with our big jobs refused to send our children to the African free schools. The African church is unfortunately what used to educate our children, not train, educate! They [the Black churches] no longer do that. They have become comfortable whore houses; but there are some who still continue, so don't give up hope, sister. What we need is a rejuvenation. We need to tell the minister in our community, if he won't preach about life, rather than death, he is going to run a cross-country mile never to come back. That is it. The church is where most of us are, let's face it, or the synagogue, or the mosque. Tell the imam, the minister, or the rabbi to shape up, and you have to make sure he does; if he doesn't, who is behind this? Cut him off. He has pimped enough on you; if he wants ten percent of your wages, let him work for it. He should tell you to prepare for life, and not death. Only a fool is prepared for death. A man who gets a new Jaguar is not prepared for death, he's preparing to drive that Jaguar. If he doesn't live by what he says, that's why nothing happens! You haven't held anybody responsible for what they are telling you.

 I would like to thank both the brothers for coming here to give us the benefit of their knowledge. I'd like to ask a question which is about today, rather than our history, because it is very important that our history is known, because we can't go forward until we know where we came from.

There are people today, African people, who feel that our future lies in having a piece of the cake, a piece of the pie, and in fact, one very esteemed brother came here and told us that we have to get involved in the police force. We've got to get to Parliament. That is not what I see as the road which we should be walking now. A lot of people who know a great deal about history are also heading in that direction, and they are telling everyone else that that's where we should be going. I feel that that would be destructive to us, to our grandchildren, to our great-grandchildren. I'd like to know from you brothers whether you would agree with us having any piece of that pie that has been stolen from us, or whether as I believe, we have to destroy, dismantle the structure that they have set up or to continue still eating the pie and start all over again, and see if we can make another pie.

Dr. Clarke: The structure is going to destroy itself. The structure is doing that. Your job is to create the atmosphere for a new human society, principally for our people. If our people benefit from it, so well and good. I don't believe that there is a capitalist solution to your problem. I do not believe there is a communist or socialist solution either, unless it is one that you shape to suit your needs. I do not believe anybody else is going to find a solution for you, but you, and I do not think it is anyone's intention or program or agenda to find a solution for you or yourself. No matter what kind of "ism" we choose, remember nothing ever came from the European mind which did not have a Christian intention, the facilitation of European control over the world. And once you are clear about that you will know what you have to do. Take anything you think you can use, Christianity, Islam, Judaism, anything. But shape it to suit your needs and have no apologies after you do it.

Dr. ben-Jochannan: I think that the brother needs to sharpen his view. I will never run for office in any country, but I personally will back an individual who may want to run, provided that individual has made his dedication by action to my people, and his or her objective is the destruction of oppression. You see, it's not about going into the system. It's the purpose of going into the system. I teach at a white school, Cornell University, I've been there for fifteen years. It's the first school I haven't been fired from of forty-seven schools. And the reason why I'm not fired is because the director is an African-American, and it's not because they didn't try. But you see, brothers and sisters, to get the program I'm teaching, the students took up guns and burned down many of the buildings on the campus. I teach there from an African orientation. The system is a white system. My paycheck comes signed by a white man, and I receive that check every two weeks. But part of that check goes to the Committee of Thirteen that helps the PAC [Pan African Congress]. You see, I don't personally help the ANC [African National Congress]. They've got enough liberal help. I help those brothers and sisters that carry with them little pamphlets on Marcus Mosiah Garvey in their pockets, the PAC. Those are the brothers and sisters that say, "I'm not sharing my land with anybody."

So if the brother or sister you are talking about is obligated to the African community and you know what he is going to do; you know what kind of measures he is going to introduce. Then you go and pray to Jah. I pray, and if you see me praying, and you have done me something wrong, you have to start running, because I have never asked God for anything. I go to the Goddess. You see the people I pray to are females, because men don't come rushing out of things. I go to the sister, and say, "Mom," you know my mom died a few years ago, so I say "Mom, Goddess, they're messing with your son again." And my mother always gives me the right answer. My mother never asked me to pray. If someone hit me, she'd say, "Kill the bastard and then come back and pray to me, boy!" And then I pray and say: "... thank you for helping me."

Q I wondered if one or both of the speakers would help me with my own history. My question was actually sparked off by something Professor Clarke said when he talked about the struggle which occurred on the Guyana-Surinam border, where there still exist whole numbers of people who are African in every sense of the word. I believe around 1957, either before or after Ghana got her independence a Ghanaian called Ezie Agyare visited Guyana and many people from there spoke in a language common to themselves and their king. Am I correct in saying that there was such a king called Ezie Agyare, and if so, can you tell me some more about him and about the struggle?

Dr. Clarke: I hate to break your heart, but I knew him personally, and he was a phony. He was a Nigerian student running a con game. He was a very interesting Nigerian, and when I went to Nigeria looking for him I never got to find him, because he always got out of the city the day before I got there. There have been many true kings, but he happened not to be one of them. I happened to know the time, know the book he wrote after he came back from Guyana and know that it was a good show game, but not real.

Dr. ben-Jochannan: At the same time this doesn't say that you are talking about the "Djuka," who also call themselves "Mingre." The Mingre people fought the Dutch, won their independence, and went up in the highlands. They are still planning to build a central road which is going to impose on the people's [Mingre] culture. And they are afraid of that; and yes, they are in the bush, but remember, there was a study by two Harvard University doctors who found that these people when they have broken bones do not operate. They have bush treatment so that in twenty-four hours you can walk; and the Howard University Medical Association agreed that it happens. They went to see it but still call the practitioners witch doctors. Among the Mingre, a percentage of the population have Ph.D.'s from the best schools throughout the world. They return to their farms and hang up their diploma. They only profess to defend themselves against slicksters as a result of that phony king. We've got a new one in America who says he is the son of Selassie. And there are a lot of people in America who believe this. I went off to New Jersey to meet this brother, because I heard that he came from the northwest; so I thought that if he came from the northwest of Ethiopia he would understand my language, but he didn't. So we've got a few of those, but the Mingres are our people; they did establish their own republic, and were an independent part of colonial Dutch Guiana, which has become the Republic of Guyana.

 They say history is the best teacher. If this is so, what should we have learned from our experiences as captives of Europeans?

Dr. ben-Jochannan: We have done a lot already. One of the few things we could do is to deal with the mind. You know, it bothers me to go to Antigua at Nelson's Wharf. Lord Nelson murdered more Black people than you can imagine! We've got to stop and think about how people view us; and that we are no less than anyone else. If an Englishman could hate what a German did to him, why does the Englishman want me to love what he did to me? If he or she doesn't understand it, that is their problem. I understand it! We need to change the mind of our people. In Trinidad, a few months ago, I was there giving some lectures, and they had a big argument about changing [the name of] a street, a boulevard in Trinidad, to [honor] the first Trinidadian labor union leader, one of the strongest union men in the whole Caribbean as against Princess Anne Boulevard. Why did they have this argument in Parliament? Unless we have accepted that we are less than any other human beings, then we can't see any way other than this negative way as African people. We can't accept our inferiority by naming our children European names like Margaret, Mary, Elizabeth and John. You can find some African names that have got meaning.

Q Before I ask my question, I would like to congratulate Professor Ben because I admire him very much in referring direct questions to his elders. I would like him to respect me too. The question is that living in America and being such an excellent scholar, and achieving the highest goal, can you do something to alleviate the fears such as talking personally to your own children? George Washington left a memorial for all of us to provide an opportunity for the unfortunate, hungry, naked Black children. Now what have you done, apart from your family, to inspire us and make us participate and alleviate some of the stresses we suffer under colonialism?

Dr. ben-Jochannan: I never disobey elders, so I'm going to give you some of the things I think I've done that may be acceptable to you. In 1938 I published my first book on Africa. Since 1938 I've published thirty-two books on Africa, and I write them in such a way that even a seventh-grader should be able to read them. I also have fourteen other manuscripts and an encyclopedia of seven volumes. I established my own publishing company. We send to jails, hospitals and certain places, books free to African-Americans, African, and African-Caribbean prisoners. I teach right now at a school called Malcolm-King College and for the last eighteen years consecutively on a voluntary basis every Thursday night in the Harlem community. I go to Head Start Programs in eight public schools, at no charge, to lecture very young brothers and sisters. I frequent a place called Pan-Pan Restaurant, near the corner of West 135th Street where I live. Never has a member of the African community come to me and said, "I'm hungry," and I would not say, "Take what you want off the menu." I've got to say what I do with my children, because I've never let a child that is charged to me be in need of food, clothing and shelter.

Sir, if you ask me personally, I was a civil engineer. I worked for many projects and for many people without charge; and as a lawyer I have taken numerous cases when I was a legal practitioner for free. I have trained my children so that one of my daughters works as a physician in a clinic only two days a week for her own pocket, and then four days for the people in Puerto Rico, with one day free. Her husband does likewise. I've trained my children, first, their duty to their people. I volunteered and went to Zanzibar and fought, physically for my people. I have done the best that I can in my little life, sir.

Dr. Clarke: There is a need to create a simple literature of explanation as to what happened to us and still must happen, and that some of us and not enough of us are trying to create and make the basis of that literature. Among other things, I am a curricula specialist and adviser to the school systems, not those in New York City; it is impossible because this is a capitalist school system controlled by an ethnic group which is going to continue to control them. When Eric Huntley, who lives here and is one of the editors at Bogle-L'Ouverture, was in New York, he visited me at my home and we talked about the possibility of doing children's books. More particularly, children's books directed to the Caribbean community in England. He stated that you have really, some of you, three countries. You have the Caribbean, yours by right, because your mother and father came from there Africa by natural history belongs to you and you are fortunate, in that you have two heritage choices both African.

And I think that what we have to do among other things is to charge our writers to explain more and more our role in history, to put it in a language the ordinary people can understand. One of the main reasons why Malcolm X had so much knowledge and was listened to was that he spoke in a language that communicated to mass audiences, communicated with ordinary people. I think that we need to take the situation out of its high academic language and put it in a language that all people can understand. All people cannot be historians, but they can be readers; all people are leaders, each individual must ultimately be a leader to himself and what you have to decide is that we need and must have a revolution, a cultural revolution, a revolution of the mind. And when you look for a leader you can't look anyplace except in a mirror and look at the person staring back at you and say, "My revolution starts with me, my revolution starts right now."

Q I take this opportunity to say something, because I am South African, and a lot has been said about South Africans, and I was glad to hear what I heard from the two professors concerning Black nationalism. But we are faced with a South Africa that has got the ANC at its forefront. The ANC was a very positive movement in 1912, when it started because the Africans were still dealing in terms of tribes and they brought the tribes together. But since that time, up to the 1950s, the ANC has become very elitist. If you can't speak English in the ANC you are nobody, so that eliminates a whole heap of Africans.

I stand here to say that the PAC is not as powerful as it would like to be. The youngsters of 1976 took on the message of the PAC without even their PAC elders there, and lately we've got AZAPO [Azanian People's Organization]. They are the youngsters who are doing the revolution at home and not the ANC. I further stand here to say that inside the ANC the people who are fighting the army are Africans, all of them. There is not one Asian, there is not one colored, there is not one white. The structure of the ANC, the people who are commanding the ANC are all white and Asian with a few privileged Blacks like Tambo who are prepared to be the window dressers of the ANC and give them dignity. What I want to say to the audience today is that when you go to the ANC meetings, I don't say don't attend them, but watch out for this. The people who are in charge are either Asians or whites, with a few privileged Africans who will not dare even to speak to a fellow African in any African language, because it's been deemed tribal. The other thing that they will not do, you go inside there, and they are talking about African heroes, and the next thing you talk about is some bore who was a communist, and on an African night you will be fed Indian food. That is our ANC. Now all of you have got a choice as to who you want to support. I am not saying that you must support this part or the other party, but be aware of the fact that if you are supporting the ANC those are some of the things that you are saying, that you are fighting for tonight, those are the things you are supporting in that party.

Dr. Clarke: The sister has opened up another lecture series; it's a little too big for tonight. I have studied the history of South Africa before the ANC and have written a book on the personalities and the various wars, the whole Zulu line, and up to the last Zulu war, in 1906, the founding of the ANC, the founding of the trade union movement of Kamaka Dele and how Kamaka Dele's movement was systematically destroyed by leftists sent there to help him into destruction. This is the perfect example of the tragedy of integration. When someone is integrated into your organization they must take orders from you or get out. This is the last thing that I think has not been learned. In New York City I have been able to speak for the ANC and the PAC, and when the order came that the PAC and the ANC never sit on the same platform I knew that this was not Black folks. If they are both working for the same cause and for the liberation of Africa then they should be able to sit on the same platform. This is white infiltration in order to facilitate white control.

Dr. ben-Jochannan: My sister, you couldn't speak better for me, and in the African tradition the youth leads the elders also. I go back to when one of the founders of the early ANC came to the United States, and I personally supported him out of my pocket. I too switched. You see when I meet a man of the ANC and he calls me "comrade," I say, "I prefer brother." And he says he can't answer "brother," because everybody in the ANC isn't necessarily brother in skin tone; so I say, "you've lost me." I remember UNDENAMO and FRELIMO [liberation movements in Mozambique]—same thing. I supported UNDENAMO against FRELIMO because UNDENAMO said, "This is my country, I am not fighting for integration. Somebody came and took my country. I am not fighting to share it with the guy that took it." England doesn't share its country with you. France doesn't share its country with you; so why should I share my country? Did England share her country with the Nazis? Why ask me to share my country with the people who invaded it? No way! Look, when it is over, and I hope that I have a few more years to be there, they owe me a pound of flesh; and I am entitled to my pound, because I've got a zeal from 1506 C.E./ A.D., that I must deal with. My ancestors in the next world will not be contented if I came back and said, "I was there when it happened!" And when they say to me: "Did you take revenge?" And I said: "No, I turned the other cheek!" What a fool I would be!

Q I would like to make a point about religion, but before I do that I heard some people asking the elder over here to apologize for the point that he raised. But it's important that we know that if he had not raised those points we would not have been able to hear the good words from the brothers. What I want to say about religion is this, if we see ourselves as African people we have to have beliefs in African religion or African way of believing in the universe and understanding creation. And we must be aware that these African beliefs in a way have been the basis for the major western religions like Islam and Christianity that exist today and that these religions exploit us, oppress us, brainwash us now. I believe that the practice of the religion will give us the African personality and mentality that we need as a basis for political, social and cultural unity. Now I think also that we should seek to get rid of Islam, Christianity and other such religions because they confuse and deprive us. I would like to hear the comments from the brother.

Dr. ben-Jochannan: I will answer that in this way. African religion serves Africans, and shouldn't be the Africans who serve it. When you must serve a religion, that religion must help you, for it must serve you. It served me to the extent that when I walked into the temple of Goddess Het-Heru (or Hathor) at Dendera and I looked up in the ceiling I knew where *God* was. I was not looking for *God*; I found *God*! In the temple they show Goddess Nut, an African woman giving birth to the sun out of her vagina. It is a picture. In most of the temples they showed God of Fertility, Min, with his penis connected to his umbilical cord out of his navel as an extension of life. In the Tomb of Pharaoh Rameses VI, in the Valley of the Kings, they show the forty-two "Admonitions of Goddess Maat," which is also called the "Negative Confessions," from whence Moses got the "Ten Commandments."

I can't help but agree with you. At least if those of us who follow other religions, and don't know the basis of that religion is our foundation, i.e., the Ten Commandments; the story of Cain and Abel which came out of the story of God Seth, who killed his brother God Osiris; shown in many temples. The most dramatic place being at the City of Edfu, the Temple of God Heru. I think that if our people knew the history and development of religion, then they may hold different views.

If all people knew Christianity and the source from whence it came (such as the story of Mary, which is 4100 years after the exact story of Goddess Aset [Auset or Isis] and the birth of her child, God Heru, and that there are sixteen such stories, the Mary-Jesus story being the last of the sixteen) then their actions towards African people (their religions and religious beliefs) would be different. If all people in Islam knew that even the Islamic Koran, and other books connected to it, speaks to the fact that Hagar who gave birth to Ishmael was an African woman. That Abraham, the first of the Jews, worshipped the Goddess Hathor (or Het-Heru) which the Bible called the "golden calf." This was after the Jews had the Kabalah. You go and look at the teachings of Pharaoh Akhnaten and see the first concept of a monotheistic God. If Judaism is based on an African religion, if Christianity is based on an African religion, and if Islam is based on an African religion, then why is the African looking outside Africa for religion? Or are you telling me that I am better than my mother? A fruit cannot be better than the tree whence it came. And Islam, Christianity and Judaism cannot deny their African past.

Dr. Clarke: I only want to add that I have a great drawback in religion, in that we first take someone's interpretation of our religion, we take carbon copies instead of our original and we never make political use of the religion. All other people make political use of their religion. All other people make political and cultural uses of religion except us, and that may be the greatest failing, in regard to religion, we give so much to it and we take so little from it.

Carole A. Parks

AN INTERVIEW WITH
YOSEF BEN-JOCHANNAN*

Yosef A. A. ben-Jochannan is a noted scholar and lecturer particularly respected for his meticulous research into the roots of African history. Born in Ethiopia, he grew up in the Caribbean and traveled extensively with his parents through Cuba, Puerto Rico and South America. He began his advanced education, which has included the University of Puerto Rico, the University of Havana, the University of Barcelona and LaSalle Extension University with the idea of becoming a civil engineer, and received degrees also in law and cultural anthropology. He came to the United States in 1945, and made New York City his home base until early 1988 when he took up residence in Cairo/Giza, Egypt.

As an East African Specialist in cultural anthropology with UNESCO, Dr. ben-Jochannan conducted research in Africa, mainly Egypt, Sudan and Ethiopia. He is well versed in Hebrew, Spanish, Potuguese, Agu (an ancient Ethiopian language), Arabic, Greek, and

---

* An interview for *Black World Magazine*, February 1974. Dr. ben-Jochannan's biographical information has been updated.

has a reading knowledge of Italian and classical German. His Harlem apartment boasts a library of approximately 12,000 books, manuscripts and rare maps (some dating back to the 15th century A.D.) Dr. Ben, as he is affectionately called, served as a Professor in Residence at El Azar University in Cairo, Egypt. He is a retired professor from Cornell University, and a former lecturer at Marymount College, and Malcolm-King College. Most of his books have been published by his own non-profit organization, Alkebu-lan Foundation, Inc. They include: *Black Man of the Nile And His Family, African Origins of the Major "Western Religions," Africa: Mother of "Western Civilization," A Chronology of the Bible: A Challenge To The Standard Version, The Black Man's Religion: Extracts and Comments From the Sacred Scriptures of The Holy Black Bible, Influence of Great Myths on Contemporary Life, Or the Need for Black History in Mental Health, The Black Man's or the "Negro's" Bicentennial Year of ??? from 1619-20 to 1976* C.E., *Our "Black Seminarians" and "Black Clergy": Without a "Black Theology," Tutankhamun's African Roots Haley, Et Al Overlooked, The African Mysteries System of Wa'set, Egypt And Its European Stepchild: "Greek Philosophy," In Pursuit of G. M. James Study of Ta-Merry's "Mysteries System," and The Ritualization of The Late Bro. Kwesie Adebisi, They All Look Alike! All?,* Vols. I, II, III, IV, *Abu Simbel-Ghizeh Guide Book/Manual,* and with George E. Simmonds, *Cultural Genocide In The Black and African Studies Curriculum.*

Dr. John Henrik Clarke

A SEARCH FOR IDENTITY

M y own search for an identity began as I think it begins
for all young people—a long time ago when I looked at
the world around me and tried to understand what it was
all about.

My first teacher was my great grandmother whom we called
"Mom Mary." She had been a slave first in Georgia and later in
Alabama where I was born in Union Springs. It was she who told us
the stories about our family and about how they had resisted slavery.
More than any other story, she told us the story of Buck, her first
husband, and how he had been sold to a man who owned a stud
farm in Virginia. Stud farms are an aspect of slavery that has been
omitted from the record and about which we do not talk any more.
We should remember, however, that there were times in this country
when slave owners used slaves to breed stronger slaves in the same
way that a special breed of horse is used to breed other horses.

My great grandmother had three children with Buck—my
grandfather Jonah, my grandaunt Liza, who was a midwife, and
another child. With Buck Mom Mary had as close to a marriage as
a slave can have—a marriage with the permission of their respective
masters. Mom Mary had a lifelong love affair with Buck, and years

later after the emancipation she went to Virginia and searched for him for three years. She never found him, and she came back to Alabama where she spent the last years of her life.

My Family

Mom Mary was the historian of our family. Years later when I went to Africa and listened to oral historians, I knew that my great grandmother was not very different from the old men and women who sit around in front of their houses and tell the young children stories of their people—how they came from one place to another, how they searched for safety, and how they tried to resist when the Europeans came to their lands.

This great grandmother was so dear to me that I have deified her in almost the same way that many Africans deify their old people. I think that my search for identity, my search for what the world was about, and my relationship to the world began when I listened to the stories of this old woman. I remember that she always ended the stories in the same way that she said "Good-bye" or "Good morning" to people. it was always with the reminder, "Run the race, and run it by faith." She did not rule out resistance as a form of obedience to God. She thought that the human being should not permit himself to be dehumanized, and her concept of God was so pure and so practical that she could see that resistance to slavery was a form of resistance to God. She did not think that any of us children should be enslaved, and she thought that anyone who had enslaved anu of of God's children had violated the very will of God.

I think Buck's pride in his manhood was the major force that made her revere her relationship with him. He was a proud man and he resisted. One of the main reasons for his master selling him to a stud farm owner was the belief that he would breed strong slaves whose wills the master would then break. This dehumanizing process was a recurring aspect of slavery.

Growing up in Alabama, my father was a brooding, landless sharecropper, always wanting to own his own land: but on my father's side of the family there had been no ownership of land at all. One day after a storm had damaged our farm and literally blown the roof off our house, he decided to take his family to a mill city—

Columbus, Georgia. He had hoped that there he would earn enough money and one day return to Alabama as an independent farmer. He pursued this dream the rest of his life. Ultimately the pursuit of this dream killed him. Now he has a piece of land, six feet deep and the length of his body; this is as close as he ever came to being an independent owner of land.

In Columbus I went to country schools, and I was the first member of the family of nine children to learn to read. I did so by picking up signs, grocery handbills, and many other things that people threw away, and by studying the signboards. I knew more about the different brands of cigarettes and what they contained than I knew about the history of the country. I would read the labels on tin cans to see where the products were made, and these scattered things were my first books.

Because I had learned to read early, great things were expected of me. I was Sunday School teacher of the junior class before I was ten years old. And I was the one person who would stop at the different homes in the community to read the Bible to old ladies. In spite of growing up in such abject poverty, I grew up in a very culturally rich environment that had its oral history and with people who not only cared for me but pampered me in many ways. I know that this kind of upbringing negates all the modern sociological explanations Black people that assume that everybody who was poor was without love. I had love aplenty and appreciation aplenty, all of which gave me a sense of self-worth that many young Black children never develop.

I began my search for my people first in the Bible, I wondered why all the characters—even those who, like Moses, were born in Africa—were white. Reading the description of Christ as swarthy and with hair like sheep's wool, I wondered why the church depicted him as blond and blue-eyed. Where was the hair like sheep's wool? Where was the swarthy complexion? I looked up the map of Africa and I knew Moses had been born in Africa. How did Moses become so white? If he went down to Ethiopia to marry Zeporah, why was Zeporah so white? Who painted the world white? then I began to search for the definition of myself and my people in relationship to world history, and I began to wonder how we had become lost from the commentary of world history.

My Teachers

In my first years in city schools in Columbus, Georgia, my favorite teacher and the one I best remember was Evelena Taylor, who first taught me to believe in myself. She took my face between her hands and looking me straight in the eyes, said, "I believe in you." It meant something for her to tell me that she believed in me, she told me what education is, and what it is supposed to do for me. These were lonely years for me. These were the years after the death of my mother—a beautiful women, a washerwoman—who had been saving fifty cents a week for my education, hoping that eventually she would be able to send her oldest son to college. Her hopes did not materialize; she died long before I was ten.

I did, however, go to school earlier than some of the other children. We lived just outside of the city limits. Children living beyond the city limits were supposed to go to country schools because the city schools charged country residents $3.75 each semester for the use of books. This was a monumental sum for us because my father made from $10.00 to $14.00 a week as a combination farmer and fire tender at the brickyards. In order to get the required $3.75 each semester, my father and some of my uncles had to put their money together. It was a collective thing to raise what was for us a large sum of money not only to send a child to a city school instead of to a country school but also to make certain that the one child in the family attending the city school had slightly better clothing than the other children. So I had a coat that was fairly warm and a pair of shoes that was supposed to be warm but really were not. As I think about the shoes, my feet sometimes get cold even now, but I could not tell my benefactors that the shoes were not keeping me warm.

As I approached the end of my last year in grammar school, Evelena Taylor told me that she would not let me use the color of my skin as an excuse for not aspiring to be true to myself and for not achieving my greatest potential. She taught me that I must prepare myself. I think my value to the field of teaching history is that I have prepared myself during my lifetime, and I have prepared myself in the years when no one was thinking of Black Studies, and I kept on preparing myself until ultimately the door opened.

I worked before and after school mostly for white people who had libraries, and children who never read books. I began to borrow books from the libraries and bring them home. In Columbus Georgia, where they had Jim Crow libraries and Black people could not use the public library, I began to forge the names of well-known white people on notes that instructed the librarian to give me a certain book. I accumulated a great many books that way. This illegitimate book borrowing went on for quite some time until one day the white person whose name I had forged appeared in the library at the same time I did. This put an end to my illegitimate use of the public library of Columbus.

I have always had a phenomenal memory. When I was a younster, I could quote verbatim much of what I had read in almancs and in encyclopedias. I became interested in writing an essay about the role of the Black man in ancient history. I went to a lawyer for whom I worked. He was a kind man whose library i had used quite extensively. Because I couldn't find any I asked him for a book on the role that Black people had played in ancient history. In a kindly way he told me that I came from a people who had no history but, that if I persevered and obeyed the laws, my people might one day make history. Then he paid me the highest compliment that a white man could pay a Black man in the period when I was growing up. He told me that one day I might grow up to be a great negro like Booker T. Washington.

At that time white people considered that the greatest achievement to which a Black man could aspire was to reach the status of the great educator, Booker T. Washington. Booker T. had been a great educator and he built up Tuskegee Institute, but he consistently cautioned his people to be patient with the Jim Crow system and to learn to be good servants and artisans. He said it was more important to earn a dollar a day (at the turn of the century that was considered good pay for the Black man) than to hope to work for or to sit next to white people in the opera. He was actually telling his people never to seek social equality. Later on he was challenged by W. E. B. DuBois, who created a whole new school of thought based on the belief that Blacks should aspire to anything they wanted, be it street-cleaner or president.

At the time of my conversation with the lawyer I had nothing for or against Booker T. Washington, I really didn't know much about the lawyer either, and his philosophy of racial equality did not mean a great deal to me. What insulted every part of me and insulted every part of me to the very depth of my being was his assumption that I came from a people without any history. At that point of my life I began systematic search for my people's role in history.

Other Influences

During my first year in high school I was doing chores and, because the new high school did not even have a cloak room, I had to hold the books and papers of a guess lecturer. The speaker had a copy of a book called *The New Negro*. Fortunately I turned to an essay written by a Puerto Rican of African descent with a German-sounding name. It was called, "The Negro Digs Up His Past." by Arthur A. Schomburg. From this essay I learned that I came from a people with a history older than the history of Europe. It was a most profound and overwhelming feeling—this great discovery that my people did have a place in history and that, indeed, their history was older than that of their oppressors.

This essay was my introduction to the ancient history of Black people. Years later when I came to New York, I started to search for Arthur Schomburg. Finally, one day I went to the 135th street library and asked a short-tempered clerk to give my letter to Mr. Schomburg. In an abrupt manner she said, "You will have to walk up three flights." And I did, and there I saw Mr. Schomburg. I told him, impatiently, that I wanted to know the history of my people, and I wanted to know it right now and in the quickest possible way. His patience more than matched my impatience. He said, "Sit down, son. What you are calling African history and Negro history is nothing but the missing pages in world history. You will have to know general history to understand these specific aspects of history." He continued patiently, "You have to study your oppressor. That's where your history got lost." Then I began to think that at last I will find out how an entire people—my people—disappeared from the respected commentary of human history.

It took time for me to learn that there is no easy way to study history. (There is, in fact, no easy way to study anything.) It is necessary to understand all the components of history in order to recognize its totality. It is similar to knowing where the tributaries of a river are in order to understand the nature of the river and to see what made the river so big. Mr. Schomburg, therefore, told me to study general history. He said, repeatedly, "Study the history of your oppressor."

I began to study the general history of Europe, and I discovered that the first rise of Europe—the Greco-Roman period—was a period when Europe "borrowed" very heavily from Africa. This early civilization depended for its very existence on what was taken from African civilization. At that time I studied Europe more than I studied Africa because I was following Mr. Schomburg's advice, and I found out how and why the slave trade started.

When I returned to Mr. Schomburg, I was ready to start a systematic study of the history of Africa. It was he who is responsible for what I am and what value I have in the field of African history and the history of Black people all over the world.

I grew to manhood in Harlem, having arrived in New York when I was seventeen. I was a depression radical—always studying, always reading, taking advantage of the fact that in New York I could go into a public library and take out books, read them, bring them back, get more books, and even renew them after a six week period. It was a joyous experience to be exposed to books. Actually, I went through a period of adjustment because my illegitimate borrowing of books from the library of Columbus, Georgia, had not prepared me to walk freely out of a library with a book without feeling like a thief. It took several years before I really felt that I have every right to go there.

During this period, in Harlem, many Black teachers were begging for Black students, but they did not have to beg me. Men like Willis N. Huggins, Charles C. Seifert, and Arthur A. Schomburg literally trained me not only to study African history and the history of Black people the world over but to teach this history.

My Teaching

All the training I received from my teachers was really set in motion by my great grandmother's telling me the stories of my family and my early attempts to search first for my identity as a person, then for the definition of my family and finally for the role of my people in the whole flow of human history.

One thing that I learned very early was that knowing history and teaching it are two different things, and the first does not necessarily prepare one for the second. At first I was an exceptionally poor teacher because I crowded too many of my facts together and they were poorly organized. I was nervous, overanxious, and impatient with my students. I began my teaching career in community centers in Harlem. However, I learned that before I could become an effective teacher, I had to gain better control of myself as a human being. I had to acquire patience with young people who giggled when they were told about African kings. I had to understand that these young people had been so brainwashed by our society that they could see themselves only as depressed beings. I had to realize that they had in many ways adjusted to their oppression and that I needed considerable patience, many teaching skills, and great love for them in order to change their attitudes. I had to learn to become a more patient and understanding human being. I had to take command of myself and understand why I was blaming people for not knowing what I knew, and blaming students for not being so well versed in history. In effect, I was saying to them, "How dare you not know this?"

After learning what I would have to do with myself and my subject matter in order to make it more understandable to people with no prior knowledge, I began to become an effective teacher. I learned that teaching history requires not only patience and love but also the ability to make history interesting to the students. I learned that the good teacher is partly an entertainer, and if he loses the attention of his class, he has lost his lesson. A good teacher, like a good entertainer, first must hold his audience's attention. Then he can teach his lesson. Then he can teach his lesson.

I taught African history in community centers in the Harlem area for over twenty years before I had any regular school assignment.

My first regular assignment was as director of the Heritage Teaching Program of Haryou-Act, an anti-poverty agency in Harlem. Here I had the opportunity to train young Black people how to approach history and to use history as an instrument of personal liberation. I taught them that taking away a people's history is a way to enslave them. I taught them that history is a two-edged sword to be used for oppression or liberation. The major point that I tried, sometimes successfully, to get across to them is that history is supposed to make one self-assured but not arrogant. It is not supposed to give one any privileges over other people, but it should make one see oneself in a new way in relation to other people.

After five years in the Haryou-Act project, I accepted my first regular assignment at Hunter College, where I remained for seventeen years. I also served as visiting professor at another university and as an instructor in Black Heritage during the summer program conducted for teachers by the history department of a third major university. I also traveled, to the extent that my schedule permitted, training teachers how to teach about Black heritage.

The Black Power explosion and the Black Studies explosion had pushed men like me to the forefront in developing approaches to creative and well-documented Black curricula. Forced to be in the center of this arena, I had to take another inventory of myself and my responsibilities. I have found young Black students eager for this history and have found many of them having doubts about whether they really had a history in spite of the the fact that they had demanded it. I have had to learn patience all over again with young people on another level.

On the college level I encountered another kind of young Black student—much older than those who giggled—the kind who does not believe in himself, does not believe in history, and who consequently is in revolt. This student says in effect, "Man, you're turning me on. You know that we didn't rule ancient Egypt." I have had to learn patience all over again as I learned to teach on a level where students come from a variety of cultural backgrounds. In all my teaching I have used as my guide the following definition of heritage, and I would like to conclude with it:

Heritage, in essence, is the means by which people have used their talents to create a history that gives them memories they can respect and that they can use to command the respect of other people. The ultimate purpose of heritage and heritage teaching is to use people's talents to develop awareness and pride in themselves so that they themselves can achieve good relationships with other people.

A READING GUIDE FOR THE STUDY AND TEACHING OF AFRICAN WORLD HISTORY

This reading guide is designed as an introduction to African world history which will stimulate a continuous study of the subject. In the thirty sessions outlined here, African history and its relationship to world history will be explained. The reading guide will start with an examination of the evidence that tends to prove that mankind originated in Africa. Special attention will be paid to all the main currents of African history such as: "Africa at the Dawn of History and the Beginning of Organized Societies," "the Early Empires of the Western Sudan, West Africa and the Grandeur of African Civilizations before the Coming of the Europeans," "the Decline of the Great Nation States of Africa and the Development of the Slave Trade, Colonialism and African Resistance."

Additional sessions will be outlined as a teacher-student seminar. Such subjects as "The Role of the Arabs in Africa," "The Role of Women in Early Independent African Nations," and a detailed study of "How and Why the Slave Trade Came" will be included.

Rationale

African history is part of world history. It is a very old part and it is a very important part. There is no way to understand world history without an understanding of African history.

A distinguished African-American poet, Countee Cullen, began his poem "Heritage" with the question: "What is Africa to me?" In order to understand Africa, we must extend the question by asking, "What is Africa to Africans?" and "What is Africa to the world?" With these questions we will be calling attention to the need for a total reexamination of African history. Considering the old approach to African history and the distortion and confusion that resulted from these approaches, a new approach to African history must begin with a new frame of reference. What exactly are we talking about?

We must be bold enough to reject such terms as "Black Africa" which presupposes that there is a legitimate "white Africa." We must reject the term "Negro Africa" and the word "Negro" and all that it implies. This word, like the concept of race and racism, grew out of the European slave trade and the colonial system that followed. It is not an African word and it has no legitimate application to African people. For more details on this matter, I recommend that you read the book *The Word Negro—Its Origin and Evil Use*, by Richard B. Moore, American Publishers, New York. In a speech on "The Significance of African History," the Caribbean-American writer, Richard B. Moore has observed:

> The significance of African history is shown, though not overtly, in the very effort to deny anything worthy of the name of history to Africa and the African peoples. This widespread, and well nigh successful endeavor, maintained through some five centuries, to erase African history from the general record, is a fact which of itself should be quite conclusive to thinking and open minds. For it is logical and apparent that no such undertaking would ever have been carried on, and at such length, in order to obscure and bury what is actually of little or no significance.

The prime significance of African history becomes still more manifest when it is realized that this deliberate denial of African history arose out of the European expansion and invasion of Africa which began in the middle of the fifteenth century. The compulsion was thereby felt to attempt to justify such colonialist conquest, domination, enslavement and plunder. Hence, this brash denial of history and culture to Africa, and indeed even to human qualities and capacity for "civilization" to the indigenous peoples of Africa.

Mr. Moore is saying, in essence, that African history must be looked at anew and seen in its relationship to world history. First, the distortions must be admitted. The hard fact is that most of what we now call world history is only the history of the first and second rise of Europe. The Europeans are not yet willing to acknowledge that the world did not wait in darkness for them to bring the light, and that the history of Africa was already old when Europe was born.

Until quite recently, it was rather generally assumed, even among well-educated persons in the West, that the continent of Africa was a great expanse of land, mostly jungle, inhabited by savages and fierce beasts. It was not thought of as an area where great civilizations could have existed or where the great kings of these civilizations could have ruled in might and wisdom over vast empires. It is true that there were some notions current about the cultural achievements of Egypt, but Egypt was conceived of as European land rather than as a country of Africa. Even if a look at an atlas or globe showed Egypt to be in Africa, the popular thought immediately saw in the Sahara a formidable barrier and a convenient division of Africa into two parts: one (north of the Sahara) was inhabited by European-like people of high culture and noble history; the other (south of the Sahara) was inhabited by dark-skinned people who had no culture, and were incapable of having done anything in their dark and distant past that could be dignified by the designation of "history." Such ideas, of course, are far from the truth, as we shall see. But it is not difficult to understand why they persisted, and unfortunately still persist, in one form or another in the popular mind.

Objective

The objective of this reading guide is to examine African history and its relationship to world history before and after the slave trade and the colonial period.

Teaching Methodology

In most cases, the instructor should develop the subject of the sessions and place the information that relates to it in proper perspective so that a meaningful discussion can follow among the students and with the instructor. In these discussions, the subject should be viewed from many sides, and a comparison should be made between what the instructor has said and what was written in the required and general references relating to the subject. In these sessions the students will be expected to participate in the discussions following the formal lecture. If there are contradictions between what is said in the required readings and what is said by the instructor, these contradictions should be the basis for a class discussion.

Relevance for the Student

This bold new look at the origin and development of African history and African people is both historical and topical. These sessions will answer some current questions, because the historical background to these questions will be looked at in a more honest and creative way. In the process of this approach to the history of African people, it is hoped that the student will take another look at world history and see how Africans relate to it.

The teacher of this subject should maintain that all history is a current event, because every event in history, in some way, still affects all mankind. In these sessions, both the instructor and the students should examine the great personalities, movements and events in history and their relevance for today.

One

AFRICA'S PLACE IN WORLD HISTORY FROM THE ORIGIN OF MAN TO 1600 A.D.

First Session

1. Why African history?
2. Why the conflict over African history?
3. The relationship of African history to world history.

Main References

Africans and Their History, by Joseph B. Harris, pp. 1-25.
African History Outlined, by Carter G. Woodson, pp. 3-19.
African History, by Phillip D. Curtin, pp. 1-12.

Suggested References

Introduction to African Civilization, by John G. Jackson, read
Introduction to the book by John H. Clarke, pp. 3-35.
African History, by Basil Davidson, pp. 1-20.

For More Extensive Study

African Origins of Civilization: Myth or Reality, by Cheikh Anta
Diop.
Civilization or Barbarism, by Cheikh Anta Diop.
Black Man of the Nile, by Yosef ben-Jochannan.
Africa: Mother of Western Civilization, by Yosef ben-Jochannan.
The African Origins of Major Western Religions, by Yosef ben-
Jochannan.
Christianity Before Christ, by John G. Jackson.
Man, God and Civilization, by John G. Jackson.

Second Session

1. Africa and the origin of man.
2. The survival achievements of early man in Africa.
3. Early migrations of men and societies within Africa.

Main References

Introduction to African Civilizations, by John G. Jackson, pp. 37-
59.
Africans and Their History, by Joseph E. Harris, pp. 26-33.
African Saga: A Brief Introduction to African History, by Stanlake
Samkange, pp. 11-34.

Suggested References

The Progress and the Evolution of Man in Africa, by L. S. B. Leakey,
pp. 1-26.
The Prehistory of Africa, by J. Desmond Clark, pp. 46-64.

Africa and the Africans, by Paul Bohannon and Phillip D. Curtin, pp. 3-35.

For More Extensive Study

The following special issues of the *Journal of African Civilization,* edited by Ivan Van Sertima:
  Africans in Early Asia
  Africans in Early Europe

Third Session

1. The beginning of organized societies in Africa.
2. The early African begins to master his environment.
3. Early migrations outside of Africa.

Main References

African Saga, by Stanlake Samkange, pp. 35-36.
The Negro, by W. E. B. DuBois, pp. 5-16.
Introduction to African Civilizations, by John G. Jackson, pp. 37-59.

Suggested References

A Guide to African History, by Basil Davidson, pp. 1-10.
The History of Africa from the Earliest Times to 1800, by Harry A. Gailey, pp. 1-41.
Civilizations of Africa: Historic Kingdoms, Empires and Cultures, by George R. Pollack, pp. 3-11.
African Contribution (Part I), by John W. Weatherwax.

For More Extensive Study

The Destruction of Black Civilization, by Chancellor Williams.
A History of Precolonial Black Africa, by Cheikh Anta Diop.

African Origins of Civilizations: Myth or Reality, by Cheikh Anta Diop.

Fourth Session

1. The southern origins of Egyptian civilization.
2. Western scholarship and the attempt to take Egypt out of Africa.
3. The Africanness of Egypt.

Main References

Introduction to African Civilizations, by John G. Jackson, pp. 60-92.

African Glory, by J.C. deGraft Johnson, pp. 8-14.

Africans and Their History, by Joseph E. Harris, pp. 34-37.

African Saga, by Stanlake Samkange, p. 47.

The Destruction of Black Civilization, by Chancellor Williams, pp. 62-100.

The Peopling of Ancient Egypt and the Deciphering of Meroitic Script, UNESCO's The General History of Africa Studies, Document 1.

General History of Africa, Document 11, see article "The Origins of the Ancient Egyptians," by Cheikh Anta Diop.

Suggested References

The Progress of Evolution of Man in Africa, by L. S. B. Leakey, pp. 27-50.

History of Africa from Earliest Times to 1800, by H. A. Gailey, pp. 1-41.

History of African Civilizations, by E. Jefferson Murphy, pp. 18-36.

For More Extensive Study

The following books by Gerald Massey:
   Ancient Egypt the Light of the World, Vols. I and II.
   The Natural Genesis, Vols. I and II.
   Gerald Massey's Lectures.

A Book of the Beginnings, Vols. I and II.
African History Notebook, by William Leo Hansberry.

Fifth Session

1. Egypt and the Golden Age.
2. New revelations about the life and genius of Imhotep.
3. The impact of Egypt on the Middle East and the Mediterranean world of early Europe.

Main References

Introduction to African Civilizations, by John G. Jackson, pp. 93-152.
The Negro, by W. E. B. DuBois, pp. 5-10.
World's Great Men of Color, by J. A. Rogers, Vol. I, pp. 38.
The Destruction of Black Civilization, by Chancellor Williams, pp. 1-35.

Suggested References

Africa in History, by Basil Davidson, Chapter 2, pp. 11-41.
Africa, Its Empires, Nations and People, by Mary Penick Motley, pp. 1-46.
A History of the African People, by Robert W. July, pp. 28-49.
A History of Egypt, by J. H. Breasted, pp. 69-95.

For More Extensive Study

A History of the Modern World, by R. R. Palmer and Joel Colton.
The Story of Africa, by Basil Davidson.
Shadow of the Third Century, by Alvin Boyd Kuhn.
Who Is This King of Glory?, by Alvin Boyd Kuhn.
The Mediterranean World in Ancient Times, by Eva Sanford.

Sixth Session

1. Egypt: The Golden Age.
2. The Pharaohs of Fire, Flowers and Thunder.
3. Ankhaten viewed in the light of the earlier and the later development of Egypt. Did we stand at the threshold of a new age of man?

Main References

The World of Africa, by W. E. B. DuBois, pp. 98-114.
World's Great Men of Color, by J. A. Rogers, pp. 38-66.
African Saga, by Stanlake Samkange, pp. 55-72.

Suggested References

A History of Egypt, by J. H. Breasted, pp. 220-319.
A History of the African People, by Robert W. July, pp. 28-49.
Great Civilizations of Ancient Africa, by Lester Brooks, pp. 28-82.

For More Extensive Study

The Ancient Egyptians and the Origin of Civilization, by G. Elliot Smith, Harper & Brothers, London/New York, 1923.
Ankhaten the Rebel Pharaoh, by Robert Silverberg, Chilton Books, Philadelphia/New York, 1964.
Rameses II, The Great Pharaoh and His Times, an exhibition in the city of Denver, by Rita E. Freed, 1987.
Africa in Antiquity, Vol. I and II, The Brooklyn Museum, 1978.

Seventh Session

1. The rise of Cush.
2. The Cushite conquest of Egypt.
3. A review of Cushite rule over Egypt.

Main References

Introduction to African Civilizations, by John G. Jackson, Chapter 3, pp. 93-125.
The Destruction of Black Civilization, by Chancellor Williams, pp. 41-57.

Suggested References

Lost Cities of Africa, by Basil Davidson, Chapter 3, pp. 23-47.
Civilizations of Africa, by G. F. Pollack, pp. 13-17.
Great Civilizations of Ancient Africa, by Lester Brooks, pp. 79-109.

For More Extensive Study

Nubia: Corridor to Africa, by Adam Smith, Princeton University Press.
The Lost Pharaohs of Nubia, by Bruce Williams.
Africa, The Wonder and the Glory, by Anna Melissa Graves.
Benvenuto Cellini Has No Prejudice Against Bronze, edited by Anna Melissa Graves, Waverly Press, Baltimore, 1942.

Eighth Session

1. Ethiopia, North Africa and the Middle East.
2. Ethiopia and the Queen of Sheba.

Main References

Introduction to African Civilizations, by John G. Jackson, Chapter 2, pp. 60-92.
The Destruction of Black Civilization, by Chancellor Williams, pp. 59-69.

Suggested References

A History of the African People, by Robert W. July, Chapter 2, pp. 28-49.
Great Civilizations of Ancient Africa, by Lester Brooks, pp. 33-40 and 230-231.
Civilization of Africa, by G. F. Pollack, pp. 11-18.
Africa in History, by Basil Davidson, pp. 11-44.

For More Extensive Study

The Wonderful Ethiopians of the Ancient Cushite Empire, by Drusilla Dunjee Houston.
Ethiopia and the Origin of Civilization, by John G. Jackson.
The Africans: A Triple Heritage, by Ali A. Mazrui.

Ninth Session

1. Egypt and Cush: End of the Golden Age.
2. The first European invasion of Africa.

Main References

African Glory, by J. C. deGraft Johnson, pp. 8-24.
World's Great Men of Color, by J. A. Rogers, pp. 94-97.
The Destruction of Black Civilization, by Chancellor Williams, pp. 71-90.

Suggested References

A New History for Schools and Colleges, by F. K. Buah, Book I, pp. 101-210.

For More Extensive Study

North African Prelude, by Galbraith Welch.

Tenth Session

1. Invaders of North Africa, general view: the Phoenicians, Greeks, Romans.
2. Africa and the Punic Wars.

Main References

African Glory, by J. C. deGraft Johnson, pp. 25-36.
World's Great Men of Color, by J. A. Rogers, pp. 94-117.

Suggested References

Africa: Its Empires, Nations and People, by Mary Penick Motley, pp. 41-51.
A New History for Schools and Colleges, by F. K. Buah, Book I, pp. 101-129.

For More Extensive Study

North African Prelude, by Galbraith Welch.

Eleventh Session

1. The impact of invaders on North Africa: A general overview.
2. The Romans in Egypt.

Main References

African Glory, by J. C. deGraft Johnson, pp. 15-24.
World's Great Men of Color, by J. A. Rogers, pp. 121-131.

Suggested References

The Lost Cities of Africa, by Basil Davidson, pp. 59-63.
A New History for Schools and Colleges, by F. K. Buah, pp. 87-88 and 134-140.

Africa: Its Empires, Nations and People, by M.P. Motley, pp. 53-69.

For More Extensive Study

North African Prelude, by Anna Melissa Graves.
The Mediterranean World in Ancient Times, by Eva Sanford.
Africa and the Modern World, by R. R. Palmer and Joel Colton, see
  chapter on "The Rise of Europe."

Twelfth Session

1. Africa and the rise of Christianity: Part I.
2. The African woman in early Christianity.
3. The negative impact of the Romans on Christianity.

Main References

African Glory, by J. C. deGraft Johnson, Chapter 3, "African Romans," pp. 25-52, and Chapter 4, "The North African Church."
Man, God and Civilization, by John G. Jackson.

Suggested References

African Glory, by J. C. deGraft Johnson, pp. 37-52.
African Saga, by Stanlake Samkange, pp. 50-54.
Africa in History, by Basil Davidson, pp. 41-69.
Africa: Its Empires, Nations and People, by M. P. Motley, pp. 53-68

For More Extensive Study

North African Prelude, by Galbraith Welch.
Africa and Africans as Seen by the Classical Writers, by William Leo
  Hansberry.
Empires in the Desert, by Robert Silverberg.
History by Herodotus, trans. by George Rawlinson.

Thirteenth Session

1. Africa and the rise of Christianity, Part II.
2. Christianity again in retrospect.

Main References

African Glory, by J. C. deGraft Johnson, pp. 37-52.

Suggested References

African Origins of the Major Western Religions, by Dr. Yosef ben-Jochannan.
Sex and Race, by J. A. Rogers, Vol. I, pp. 91-95.

For More Extensive Study

Christianity Before Christ, by John G. Jackson.
Who Is This King of Glory?, by Alvin Boyd Kuhn.
Shadow of the Third Century, by Alvin Boyd Kuhn.
Africa Mother of the Major Western Religions, by Dr. Yosef ben-Jochannan.

Fourteenth Session

1. Africa and the rise of Islam: Part I.
2. Roman misrule and the corruption of Christianity as the basis for the rise of Islam.
3. The African personality in the making of Islam.

Main References

African Glory, by J. C. deGraft Johnson, pp. 37-57.

Suggested References

The Horizon History of Africa, edited by Alvin M. Josephy, Jr., Chapter IV, "The Spread of Islam," by John R. Willis, pp. 137-149.
The Dawn of African History, edited by Roland Oliver, pp. 30-36.
A New History for Schools and Colleges, by F. K. Buah, pp. 141-172.

For More Extensive Study

Story of the Moors in Spain, by Stanley Landtpoole.
Slavery and Muslim Society in Africa, by Allan G. B. Fisher and Humphrey J. Fisher.
Islam in Africa, by James Kritzeck and William H. Lewis.
Moorish Spain, by Enrique Sordo.

Fifteenth Session

1. Africa and the rise of Islam: Part II.
2. The conquest of North Africa and Spain.

Main References

African Glory, by J. C. deGraft Johnson, pp. 53-76.
Introduction to African Civilizations, by John G. Jackson, Chapter 4, pp. 157-193.

Suggested References

A New History for Schools and Colleges, by F. K. Buah, pp. 148-155.
World's Great Men of Color, by J. A. Rogers, pp. 138-171.
Man, God and Civilization, by John G. Jackson, pp. 263-283.

For More Extensive Study

North African Prelude, by Galbraith Welch.
The Mediterranean World in Ancient Times, by Eva Sanford.

New General History of Africa, Vol. I, UNESCO.

Sixteenth Session

1. The rise of Ancient Ghana.
2. The formation of Ancient Ghana.

Main References

Topics in West African History, by Adu Boahen, pp. 3-8.
African Glory, by J. C. deGraft Johnson, pp. 77-91.
African Heroes and Heroines, by Carter G. Woodson, pp. 25-31.
Introduction to African Civilizations, by John G. Jackson, pp. 196-219.

Suggested References

History of West Africa to the Nineteenth Century, by Basil Davidson, pp. 27-49.
Horizon History of Africa, edited by Alvin M. Josephy, Jr., Chapter V, "Kingdoms of the West Africa," pp. 177-185.

For More Extensive Study

A History of West Africa, by Jacob Ajayi and Michael Crowder.
Topics in West African History, New Edition, by Adu Boahen with Jacob Ajayi and Michael Tidy.
How Europe Underdeveloped Africa, by Walter Rodney.
History of West Africa, Vol. I and II, edited by J. F. Ajayi and Michael Crowder.

Seventeenth Session

1. Sundiata, spiritual father of Mali.
2. The rise of Mali.
3. Mali and the reign of Mansa Musa.

Main References

Topics in West African History, by Adu Boahen, pp. 13-17.
African Glory, by J. C. deGraft Johnson, pp. 92-99.
African Heroes and Heroines, by Carter G. Woodson, pp. 25-36.
African Saga, by Stanlake Samkange, pp. 122-135.

Suggested References

History of West Africa, by Basil Davidson, pp. 52-60.
Ancient African Kingdoms, by Margaret Shinnie, pp. 56-73.
The Dawn of African History, edited by Roland Oliver, pp. 37-43.
"Africa's Golden Past," by William Leo Hansberry, Part IV, *Ebony Magazine,* March 1965.

For More Extensive Study

A Tropical Democracy, by Flora Shaw Lugard.
Travels and Discoveries in North and in Central Africa, by Heinrich Barth.
A History of Precolonial Black Africa, by Cheikh Anta Diop.

Eighteenth Session

1. The emergence of Sunni Ali.
2. The rise of Songhay.
3. Prefaces to greatness.

Main References

Topics in West African History, by Adu Boahen, pp. 23-32.
African Heroes and Heroines, by Carter G. Woodson, pp. 37-47.
World's Great Men of Color, Vol. I, by J. A. Rogers, p. 235.

Suggested References

A History of the African People, by Robert W. July, pp. 65-70.

African History, by Basil Davidson, pp. 83-90.
African Saga, by Stanlake Samkange, pp. 136-147.
Ancient African Kingdoms, by Margaret Shinnie, pp. 73-86.

For More Extensive Study

Great Rulers of the African Past, by L. Dobler and W. A. Brown.
A Tropical Dependency, by Flora Shaw Lugard.
The Horizon History of Africa, edited by Alvin M. Josephy, Jr.
General History of Africa, Vol. IV, UNESCO.

Nineteenth Session

1. Trade and commerce during the administration of Muhammed Abubakr El-Touri.
2. The career of Muhammed Abubakr El-Touri, known as Askia the Great.
3. The administration of the Songhay Empire by El-Touri.

Main References

Topics in West African History, by Adu Boahen, pp. 23-37.
African Glory, by J. C. deGraft Johnson, pp. 100-109.

Suggested References

Great Rulers of the African Past, by L. Dobler and W. A. Brown, pp. 120-124.
Discovering our African Heritage, by Basil Davidson, pp. 98-104.
A History of West Africa, by Basil Davidson, pp. 65-72.

For More Extensive Study

History of West Africa, by Jacob Ajayi.
A Tropical Dependency, by Flora Shaw Lugard.
Lost Cities of Africa, by Basil Davidson.

Twentieth Session

1. The last years of the reign of Sunni Ali.
2. The Songhay Empire: The death of Askia the Great.
3. Songhay: Beginning of the troubled years.

Main References

Topics in West African History, by Adu Boahen, pp. 32-37.
African Background Outlined, by Carter G. Woodson, pp. 65-73.

Suggested References

History of West Africa, by Basil Davidson, pp. 19-130.

For More Extensive Study

A Tropical Dependency, by Flora Shaw Lugard.
Great Rulers of the African Past, by L. Dobler and W. A. Brown.
History of West Africa, edited by J. F. Ajayi and Michael Crowder.

Twenty-First Session

1. The significance of the year 1492: The historical background to the slave trade.

Main References

African Glory, by J. C. deGraft Johnson, pp. 153-165.
African Background Outlined, by Carter G. Woodson, pp. 217-255.

Suggested References

Introduction to African Civilizations, by John G. Jackson, read the Introduction.

For More Extensive Study

Four Centuries of Portuguese Expansion, by C. R. Boxer.
The Horizon History of Africa, by Alvin M. Josephy, Jr.
A Tropical Dependency, by Flora Shaw Lugard.

Twenty-Second Session

1. The significance of the year 1492: The second rise of Europe.
2. Gold as a factor before slavery.
3. The Elmina Castle Incident: 1482.

Main References

Topics in West African History, by Adu Boahen, pp. 102-112.
African Glory, by J. C. deGraft Johnson, pp. 120-126.

Suggested References

History of the African People, by Robert W. July, pp. 148-156.

For More Extensive Study

A History of the Gold Coast and Ashanti, by W.W. Claridge.
Ghana the Morning After, by K. Budu-Acquah.
Capitalism and Slavery, by Eric Williams.
Documents on West Indian History, by Eric Williams.

Twenty-Third Session

1. How and why the slave trade: The first impact of the Portuguese.
2. African reaction to the Portuguese.

Main References

African Glory, by J. C. deGraft Johnson, pp. 127-133.
Topics in West African History, by Adu Boahen, pp. 103-112.

Suggested References

History of West Africa, by Basil Davidson, pp. 293-298.

For More Extensive Study

Black Mother: The Slave Trade, by Basil Davidson.
Slavery and Social Death, by Orlando Patterson.

Twenty-Fourth Session

1. The Portuguese in the Congo.
2. The failure of a partnership. Why?
3. The aftermath of the failure.

Main References

A History of African People, by Robert W. July, pp. 148-156.

Suggested References

Portugal in Africa, by James Duffy, Penguin African Library, Baltimore, 1963, pp. 25-46.

For More Extensive Study

Four Centuries of Portuguese Expansion, by C. R. Boxer.
Daily Life in the Kingdom of the Kongo (From the 16th to the 18th Centuries), by Georges Balandier.
Political Awakening in the Belgian Congo (The Politics of Fragmentation), by Rene Lemarchand.

Twenty-Fifth Session

1. The Portuguese conquest of Angola.
2. Encounter with Nzingha.
3. Nzingha's resistance to Portuguese rule.

Main References

African Glory, by J. C. deGraft Johnson, pp. 254-290.

Suggested References

Portugal in Africa, by James Duffy, pp. 25-72.
Four Centuries of Portuguese Expansion, by C. R. Boxer.

For More Extensive Study

World's Great Men of Color, by J. A. Rogers.
The Portuguese Conquest of Angola, by David Birmingham.
Trade and Conflict in Angola, by David Birmingham.

Twenty-Sixth Session

1. East African slave trade.
2. Islamic rationale for the slave trade.
3. The Arab treatment of the slaves.

Main References

African Glory, by J. C. deGraft Johnson, pp. 144-150.

Suggested References

A History of East and Central Africa, by Basil Davidson, pp. 112-144.
Portugal in Africa, by James Duffy, pp. 25-72.

For More Extensive Study

The General History of Africa, Vol. VII, UNESCO.
Documents II: Slavery in the Indian Ocean, UNESCO.

Twenty-Seventh Session

1. African slave trade and the settlement of the New World.
2. Africa before the Atlantic slave trade.
3. Arab slave trade as preface to the Atlantic slave trade.

Main References

History of the African People, by Robert W. July, pp. 148-168.
Africa in History, by Basil Davidson, pp. 60-94.

Suggested References

History of West Africa, by J. D. Fage, pp. 111-132.

For More Extensive Study

Capitalism and Slavery, by Eric Williams.
The Sociology of Slavery, by Orlando Patterson.
The General History of Africa, Vol. VII, UNESCO.

Twenty-Eighth Session

1. The collapse of Western Sudan.
2. The politics of Morocco before the invasion.
3. The invasion itself.
4. The aftermath.

Main References

Topics in West African History, by Adu Boahen, pp. 32-37.

A History of the African People, by Robert W. July, pp. 63-69.
Introduction to African Civilizations, by John G. Jackson.

Suggested References

Introduction to African Civilizations, by John G. Jackson, pp. 296-360.

For More Extensive Study

The Lost Cities of Africa, by Basil Davidson.
Realm of the Evening Star: Morocco and the Land of the Moors, by Eleanor Hoffman.
Timbuctoo the Mysterious, by Felix DuBois.

Twenty-Ninth Session

1. Africa and the world, 1600 A.D.

Thirtieth Session

Seminar: Review of all previous sessions.

Two

AFRICA'S PLACE IN WORLD HISTORY FROM 1600 A.D. TO THE PRESENT

T his guide is designed as an introduction to the history of modern Africa. It is Part II of a survey of African history beginning with the origin of man to 1600 A.D.

Rationale

This guide is a general survey of African history and its relationship to the history of the rest of the world. The guide will emphasize an Africentric point of view, using a large number of books and documents by Europeans which tend to prove that the generally accepted European view of African history and African civilizations is wrong. This view of the African people was created to justify the slave trade and the colonial system. I have also used a large number of books and documents prepared by African writers and writers of African descent in the United States and in the West Indies.

Further, the presentation of this guide is intended to prove that an Africentric view of history if academically defendable. In this case, it is mainly from the view of the victim of its distortion. The restoration of African history and civilization as a part of world history and civilization is a meaningful contribution to future human relations.

Relevance for Students

In this guide the students will be participating in an examination of the prefaces to modern African history. They will be exposed to a large number of references and documents, good and bad. Further, they will examine the events and personalities that shaped African history and be able to see that these events are current in many ways. The period covered by the guide will afford the students the opportunity to learn how the slave system evolved into the colonial system and how the labor of the Africans and Asians helped to develop the economic system called capitalism. The admission or denial of African history was a major factor in this protracted crime against most of mankind.

First Session

1. The impact of the Moroccan invasion on the cultural life of Songhay and its effect on West Africa in general.
2. The nature of the resistance to Moroccan rule during the occupation of the western Sudan.
3. The intellectual destruction of the western Sudan; the exiling of the scholars.

Main References

Topics in West African History, by Adu Boahen, pp. 13-21.
Dawn of African History, by Roland Oliver, pp. 60-67.

Suggested References

Ancient African Kingdoms, by Margaret Shinnie, pp. 43-66.
History of West Africa, Vol. I, edited by J. F. Ade Ajayi and Michael Crowder, pp. 441-483.
The Horizon History of Africa, edited by Alvin M. Josephy, Jr., pp. 359-464.

For More Extensive Study

Lost Cities of Africa, by Basil Davidson.
History of West Africa, Vols. I and II, edited by J. F. Ade Ajayi and Michael Crowder.
Timbuctoo the Mysterious, by Felix Dubois.

Second Session

1. Commercial trading before the slave trade.
2. The troubled years of African civilization: the first impact of the slave trade.
3. African reaction to the slave trade and the coming of the Europeans.

Main References

African Background Outlined, by Carter G. Woodson, pp. 217-225.
African Glory, by J. C. DeGraft Johnson, pp. 151-165.

Suggested References

A History Of West Africa, by Basil Davidson, pp. 293-298.
The Horizon History of Africa, edited by Alvin M. Josephy, Jr., pp.
304-351 and 352-399.

For More Extensive Study

Topics In West African History, by Adu Boahen, see chapter "The
Coming of the Europeans."
Black Mother: The African Slave Trade, "Pre-colonial History, 1450-
1850," by Basil Davidson.
Capitalism and Slavery, by Eric Williams.

Third Session

1. The slave trade and competition among European nations for
areas of influence in Africa.
2. The slave trade and the origins of African underdevelopment.
3. The slave trade and the destruction of African culture and images.

Main References

Topics in West African History, by Adu Boahen, pp. 103-133.
African Glory, by J. C. DeGraft Johnson, pp. 151-165.
How Europe Underdeveloped Africa, by Walter Rodney, pp. 40-124.
The Slave Trade and Slavery, edited by John Henrik Clarke and
Vincent Harding, pp. 10-21.

Suggested References

African Mother: The Slave Trade, by Basil Davidson.

For More Extensive Study

The Horizon History of Africa, edited by Alvin M. Josephy, Jr.
History of West Africa, Vol. I, edited by J. F. Ade Ajayi and Michael
   Crowder.

Fourth Session

1. Nations and civilizations of the Congo and Southwest Africa: the
   struggle against the Portuguese influence.
2. The Portuguese in Mbundu, that later became Angola.
3. The aftermath of the partnership that failed.

Main References

World's Great Men of Color, by J. A. Rogers, pp. 247-250.
The Destruction of Black Civilization, by Chancellor Williams, pp.
   157-171.

Suggested References

The Horizon History of Africa, edited by Alvin M. Josephy, Jr., pp.
   69-75.
Dawn of African History, by Roland Oliver, pp. 69-75.
Portugal in Africa, by James Duffy, pp. 25-46.

For More Extensive Study

Four Centuries of Portuguese Expansion, by C. R. Boxer.
The Portuguese Conquest of Angola, by David Birmingham.
Trade and Conflict in Angola, by David Birmingham.

Fifth Session

1. Nations and civilizations of East and Central Africa: the precolonial period.

2. The coming of the Portuguese to East Africa.
3. Arab-Portuguese partnership in the slave trade.

Main References

How Europe Underdeveloped Africa, by Walter Rodney, pp. 103-261.
African Glory, by J. C. deGraft Johnson, pp. 144-150.

Suggested References

The Horizon History of Africa, edited by Alvin M. Josephy, Jr., pp.
  368-371.
History of East and Central Africa, by Basil Davidson, pp. 1-56.

For More Extensive Study

The Cambridge History of Africa, edited by Roland Oliver.
The General History of Africa, Vol. VII, UNESCO.
UNESCO Document 11: *Slavery In The Indian Ocean.*

Sixth Session

1. The formation of nations in southern Africa from the death of
   Shaka to the last Zulu War in Natal, 1906.
2. The Zulus after the death of Shaka.

Main References

African Heroes and Heroines, by Carter G. Woodson, pp. 148-166.
World's Great Men of Color, by J. A. Rogers, pp. 265-275, 287-293,
  and 363-369.

For More Extensive Study

The Zulu Aftermath, by J. Omar-Cooper.
Emperor Shaka the Great, by Mazisi Kunene.
The Zulu Kings, by Brian Roberts.

Shaka, King of the Zulus, by Daniel Cohen.
Amazulu, by Thomas B. Jenkinson.

Seventh Session

1. The people of Ghana from the rise of the Ashanti during the reign of Osei Tutu, early in the 18th century to the exiling of King Prempah in 1896.
2. The people of Ghana from 1896 (the year King Prempah was exiled) to 1900 when the Yaa Asantewa led the Ashanti people in the last of the Ashanti wars.
3. The culture consequence of the Ashanti War.

Main References

Topics in West African History, by Adu Boahen, pp. 53-76.
An Active History of Ghana, Book I and II, by Godfrey N. Brown and Philip M. Amonoo.
Ghana: A Historical Interpretation, by J. D. Fage.
The Ashanti of Ghana, by Sonia Bleeker.
Ghana: End of an Illusion, by Bob Fitch and Mary Oppenheimer.
Ancient Ghana and Mali, by Nehemia Levtzion.

Suggested References

A History of West Africa, by Basil Davidson, pp. 129-152.
World's Great Men of Color, by J. A. Rogers, pp. 142-144 and 254-263.
Ashanti Heroes, by K. O. Bonsu Kveretwie, pp. 50-54.

For More Extensive Study

A History of the Gold Coast and Ashanti, by W. W. Claridge.
A History of the Gold Coast and Asante, by Carl S. Reindorf.
Gold Coast Native Institutions, by E. Casely Hayford.
Fanti Customary Lore, by John Mensah Sarbah.

Eighth Session

1. The people of Nigeria: Culture and transition on the North from the collapse of the western Sudan to the end of the Fulani Wars.
2. The impact of the Fulani Wars on northern Nigeria.
3. Culture and religion in conflict.

Main References

Topics in West African History, by Adu Boahen, pp. 23-28 and 90-94.
The African Genius, by Basil Davidson, pp. 279-287.

Suggested References

Growth of African Civilization: The Revolutionary Years, by Webster, et.al., pp. 3-14.
The Horizon History of Africa, edited by Alvin M. Josephy, Jr.

For More Extensive Study

A History of Modern Nigeria, by Michael Crowder.
The Sword of Truth: The Life of Usman, by Dan Fodio.

Ninth Session

1. The people of Nigeria: Culture and transition among the Yorubas and the Ibos in the nineteenth century.
2. The career of Jaja and the start of Nigerian nationalism.
3. The politics of exile in Nigeria.

Main References

Topics in West African History, by Adu Boahen, pp. 90-94.

Suggested References

A History of West Africa, by Basil Davidson, pp. 135-146.
A Thousand Years of West African History, by J. F. Ade Ajayi and Espiel Ian, pp. 186-200.
The Horizon History of Africa, edited by Alvin M. Josephy, Jr., pp. 448-495.

For More Extensive Study

A History of West Africa, by Basil Davidson.
Trade and Politics in the Niger Delta, 1830-1885, by K. Omwuku Dike.
Revolution and Power Politics in Yorubaland, 1840-1893, by S. A. Akintoye.
Nigeria: Background to Nationalism, by James S. Coleman.

Tenth Session

1. The people, the cultures and the resistance movements in West Africa at the end of the nineteenth century: Samory Toure of Guinea and King Behazin of Dahomey.
2. The beginning of a new political elite in West Africa.
3. The politics of exile.

Main References

Pan-Africanism or Communism, by George Padmore, pp. 54-101
World's Great Men of Color, by J. A. Rogers, pp. 328-349.

Suggested References

Protest and Power in Black Africa, edited by Robert I. Rotberg and Ali A. Mazrui, pp. 37-80 and 512-571.

For More Extensive Study

Nigeria: Background to Nationalism, by James S. Coleman.
Trade and Politics in the Niger Delta, 1830-1885, by K. Onwuku Dike.
A History of Modern Nigeria, by Michael Crowder.

Eleventh Session

1. Resistance movements in the Sudan and along the East Coast of Africa at the end of the nineteenth century. The Mahdi (Mohammed Ahmed) Period in the Sudan and the period of Sayed Mohammed Abdullah Hassen in Somalia.
2. Political movements in East and in Central Africa.
3. The role of Islam in East and Central African revolts.

Main References

World's Great Men of Color, by J. A. Rogers, pp. 295-309.

Suggested References

World's Great Men of Color, by J. A. Rogers, pp. 178-183.
African Heroes and Heroines, by Carter G. Woodson, pp. 79-82.
Tarikh, Vol. I, No. 2, "African Leadership" (read entirely).
Tarikh, Vol. II, No. 3, "Six Aspects of African History" (read entirely).

For More Extensive Study

Fire and Sword in the Sudan, by Slatin Pasha.
A Short History of the Sudan, by Mandour el Mahdi.
The Fighting Sudanese, by H. C. Jackson.
A History of the Sudan to 1821, by A. J. Arkell.

Twelfth Session

1. Africa at the end of the nineteenth century: An overview.
2. The development of the African National Congress and other non-military resistance movements in southern Africa.
3. The birth of South African trade unionism.

Main References

Pan-Africanism or Communism, by George Padmore, pp. 268-357.
Topics in West African History, by Adu Boahen, pp. 146-155.
Tarikh, Vol. I, No. 4, "Modernizers in Africa"; Vol. II, No. 2, "African Achievement and Tragedy;" Vol. II, No. 3, "Six Aspects of African History;" and Vol. II, No. 4, "France in Africa"

Suggested References

How Europe Underdeveloped Africa, by Walter Rodney, pp. 223-287.

For More Extensive Study

Time Longer Than Rope, by Robert Roux.

Thirteenth Session

1. The twentieth-century consequences of the so-called "Scramble for Africa."
2. The consequences of the so-called "scramble" in other parts of Africa.
3. Was this the beginning or the end of the scramble for Africa?

Main References

The Destruction of Black Civilization, by Chancellor Williams, pp. 207-222.
Pan-Africanism or Communism, by George Padmore, pp. 164-204.

Suggested References

How Europe Underdeveloped Africa, by Walter Rodney, pp. 261-287.

For More Extensive Study

The Black Man's Burden, by E. D. Morel.
King Leopold's Congo, by Ruth Slade.
King Leopold's Rule in Africa, by E. D. Morel.
Red Rubber, by E. D. Morel.

Fourteenth Session

1. The rise of political movements in Africa.
2. The impact of the First World War on Africa.
3. Colonialism and contradiction.

Main References

Pan-Africanism or Communism, by George Padmore, pp. 54-115.
How Europe Underdeveloped Africa, by Walter Rodney, pp. 223-287.

Suggested References

Africans and Their History, by Joseph E. Harris, pp. 138-182.

For More Extensive Study

History of West Africa, Vol. I and II, edited by J. F. Ade Ajayi and
   Michael Crowder
Renascent Africa, by Nuamdi Azikiwe.

Fifteenth Session

1. The Independence Explosion and the impact of Africa on our
time.

2. The consequences of the explosion within Africa.
3. The consequences of the explosion abroad.
4. The consequences of the explosion on the economy of Europe.

Main References

Africa Must Unite, by Kwame Nkrumah.
Ghana: The Autobiography of Kwame Nkrumah, by Kwame Nkrumah.
Neo-Colonialism: The Last Stage of Imperialism, by Kwame Nkrumah.

Suggested References

Which Way Africa, by Basil Davidson.
Can Africa Survive?, by Basil Davidson.
Report on Southern Africa, by Basil Davidson.
The African Awakening, by Basil Davidson.

For More Extensive Study

The First Dance of Freedom, by Martin Meredith.
Marcus Garvey and the Vision of Africa, edited by John Henrik Clarke.
Dark Days in Ghana, by Kwame Nkrumah.

Sixteenth Session

Seminar: Africa Here and Now.

Main References

Africans and Their History, by Joseph E. Harris, pp. 133-216.
Pan-Africanism or Communism, by George Padmore, pp. 268-418.

Suggested References

Current newspapers and magazine articles about Africa.

Three

AFRICA'S PLACE IN AFRICAN-AMERICAN HISTORY FROM SLAVERY TO EMANCIPATION

T his reading guide was developed as a survey of the historical experience of the African people in the United States from the pre-Columbian presence to the period of the Reconstruction, beginning with the African background. This is the first part of a two-part reading guide designed for undergraduates and teachers.

Academic Objective

The intent of this reading guide is to examine, in detail, the role that the people of African descent have played in the making of the nations in what is called the "New World." Considerable time will be used to show that all the Africans who were brought to the "New World" were not slaves. In fact, some were explorers, paid sailors and soldiers, freebooters and skilled craftsmen.

Further, it will be shown that the forced labor of the Africans helped to lay the basis for the economic system called capitalism. These Africans have always been a part of "New World" history and are now a determining factor in that history.

This reading guide will reveal that the phrase, "New World" is highly questionable in the light of the old and new evidence that tends to prove that people of African descent were in large parts of North and South America and the Caribbean Islands long before Christopher Columbus opened up this part of the world for European settlement. This reading guide is presented from an Africentric point of view, using mainly the books and documents of writers of African descent in all cases where this material is available.

New information, by both Black and white writers, that proves beyond question that people of African descent have had a pre-Columbian presence in what is called the "New World," will be introduced into the reading guide. Such new works as *Introduction to African Civilizations,* by John G. Jackson (1970), and *The Art of Terracotta Pottery in Pre-Columbian Central and South America,* by Alexander Von Wathenau (1970), will be examined with students' participation. In-depth magazine articles on this subject, such as "The Beginning of the African Diaspora: Black Men in Ancient and Medieval America," parts I and II, by Legrand H. Clegg (in a bibliography in *African Affairs,* Vol. 2, Nos. 11 and 12, November and December 1969), will also be examined. A comparison will be made between these works and an earlier study of this subject by Professor Leo Wiener in his massive three volumes of research entitled *Africa in the Discovery of America* (1920).

Academic Need

African-American history is an important part of the history of the United States and the settlement of what is referred to as the "New World." This reading guide is designed for any student who wishes to make a serious study of this subject and is prepared to do the extensive reading required. In my opinion, if African-American history is important enough to be read by any student, it is important enough to be read by all students.

Teaching Methodology

This reading guide will develop the subjects of the session and place them in proper perspective so that a meaningful discussion can follow among the students and the instructor. In these discussions, the subject will be viewed from many sides, and a comparison will be made between what the instructor has said and what was written in the required and general reference relating to the subject.

First Session

1. The African basis of world history.
2. West African coastal states during the early part of the fifteenth century.
3. European positive entry and negative results.

Main References

Before the Mayflower, by Lerone Bennett, Jr., pp. 3-28.
America's Black Past, edited by Eric Foner, pp. 1-27.

Suggested References

Breaking the Chains of Bondage, by Norman E. W. Hodges, pp. 1-24.
The Negro, by W. E. B. DuBois, Chapters 1-4, pp. 5-35.
Topics in West African History, by Adu Boahen, pp. 3-28.
The Chronological History of the Negro in America, edited by Peter M. Bergman and Mort N. Bergman, pp. 1-9.
A People Uprooted 1500-1800, edited by Benjamin Quarles and Sterling Stuckey, Vol. I, pp. 7-35.

For More Extensive Study

The Horizon History of Africa, edited by Alvin M. Josephy, Jr.
West Africa, by J. F. Ajayi.
A History of West Africa to the 19th Century, by Basil Davidson and F. K. Bush.

Second Session

1. How and why African people were lost from the pages of world history.
2. The European control of image.
3. The European control of the concept of God.

Main References

The Slave Trade and Slavery, edited by John Henrik Clarke and Vincent Harding, pp. 1-9.
A People Uprooted 1500-1800, edited by Benjamin Quarles and Sterling Stuckey, Vol. I, pp. 6-69.

Suggested References

The Negro in Our History, by Carter G. Woodson and Charles H. Wesley, pp. 1-52.
The Chronological History of the Negro in America, edited by Peter M. Bergman and Mort N. Bergman, pp. 1-31.

For More Extensive Study

How Europe Underdeveloped Africa, by Walter Rodney.
The Betrayal of the Negro, by Rayford Logan.
Up from Slavery, by Booker T. Washington.

Third Session

1. The slave trade begins.
2. The role the Africans played or did not play in the slave trade.
3. The slave trade in the economic recovery of Europe.

Main References

The Slave Trade and Slavery, edited by John Henrik Clarke and Vincent Harding, pp. 1-9.
The Negro in the Making of America, by Benjamin Quarles, pp. 15-32.
Pioneers and Planters: Black Beginnings in America, by Joseph E. Penn and Earl E. Thorpe, pp. 3-11.

Suggested References

Capitalism and Slavery, by Eric Williams, pp. 3-29.
How Europe Underdeveloped Africa, by Walter Rodney, pp. 84-101.

For More Extensive Study

The Shaping of Black America, by Lerone Bennett, Jr.
Before the Mayflower, by Lerone Bennett, Jr..
Long Memory, The Black Experience in America, by Mary Frances Berry and John W. Blassingame.

Fourth Session

1. The impact of the Africans on the "New World," Part I, The pre-Columbian presence.
2. New books and new theories on the pre-Columbian presence of Africans in the Americas.
3. The economic factor of the presence of the Africans in America.

Main References

From Slavery to Freedom, by John Hope Franklin, pp. 3-10.
The Slave Trade and Slavery, edited by John Henrik Clarke and Vincent Harding,, pp. 10-17.

Suggested References

Introduction to African Civilizations, by John G. Jackson, pp. 232-260.

For More Extensive Study

They Came Before Columbus, by Ivan Van Sertima.
World's Great Men of Color, Vol. II, by J. A. Rogers.
The Negro in Our History, by Carter G. Woodson and Charles H. Wesley.

Fifth Session

1. The impact of the Africans on the "New World," Part II: The African explorers.
2. The Africans in the "New World" who were not slaves.

Main References

The Slave Trade and Slavery, edited by John Henrik Clarke and Vincent Harding, pp. 10-32.
Capitalism and Slavery, by Eric Williams, pp. 3-29.

Suggested References

Before the Mayflower, by Lerone Bennett, Jr., pp. 3-47.
Pioneers and Planters: Black Beginnings in America, by Joseph E. Penn and Earl E. Thorpe, last three chapters.
Blacks in America: Then and Now, by Edgar A. Tappin, pp. 1-8.
Great Negroes Past and Present, by Russell L. Adams, pp. 15-16.

For More Extensive Study

The Slave Community, by John W. Blassingame.
There Is a River, by Vincent Harding.
Long Memory, The Black Experience in America, by Mary Frances Berry and John W. Blassingame.

Sixth Session

1. The impact of the Africans on the "New World," Part III: Extension of the slave trade.
2. The scramble for white labor in Europe. The conditions behind the scramble. What Europeans were being enslaved, how and why.

Main References

The Slave Trade and Slavery, edited by John Henrik Clarke and Vincent Harding, pp. 1-18.
A People Uprooted 1500-1800, edited by Benjamin Quarles and Sterling Stuckey, Vol. I, pp. 37-44.

Suggested References

Capitalism and Slavery, by Eric Williams, pp. 3-50.
Early America 1492-1812, by William Loren Katz, pp. 1-7.

For More Extensive Study

The Shaping of Black America, by Lerone Bennett, Jr., Chapters 1 and 2.
Slavery and Social Death, by Orlando Patterson.

Seventh Session

1. Red servitude, Black servitude, the destruction of the Indians and their replacement by the Africans.
2. The distribution of the (so-called) Indians. A further preparation for the extension of the African slave trade.
3. Slavery and the planting of American racism.

Main References

Pioneers and Planters: Black Beginnings in America, by Joseph E. Penn and Earl E. Thorpe, pp. 3-17.
The Chronological History of the Negro in America, edited by Peter M. Bergman and Mort N. Bergman, pp. 1-13.
A People Uprooted 1500-1800, edited by Benjamin Quarles and Sterling Stuckey, Vol. I, pp. 37-51.

Suggested References

Early America 1492-1812, by William Loren Katz, pp. 1-11.
The Shaping of Black America, by Lerone Bennett, Jr., pp. 61-80.
History of Black Americans, by Philip S. Foner, pp. 95-113.

For More Extensive Study

The Slave Community, by John Blassingame.
Slavery and the Period of Revolution, by David Brian.
Slavery and Western Civilization, by David Brian.
The Caribbean: From Columbus to Castro, by Eric Williams.

Eighth Session

1. The year 1619 and the beginning of Black slavery in the United States. What manner of slavery was this?
2. The slavery system developed slowly, why?
3. White servitude: A neglected factor in slavery.

Main References

Before the Mayflower, by Lerone Bennett, Jr., pp. 29-74.
America's Black Past, edited by Eric Foner, pp. 50-74.
From Slavery to Freedom, by John Hope Franklin, pp. 40-59.

Suggested References

America's Black Past, edited by Eric Foner, pp. 75-111.
The Shaping of Black America, by Lerone Bennett, Jr., pp. 61-80.
The Slave Community, by John H. Blassingame, pp. 1-40.

For More Extensive Study

The Burden of Southern History, by C. Vann Woodward.
The Mind of the South, by Wilbur Joseph Cash.

Ninth Session

1. American independence and American slavery after the Revolution.
2. The Founding Fathers: Did they really mean what they said?
3. Liberty, death and slavery.

Main References

From Slavery to Freedom, by John Hope Franklin, pp. 126-144.
Before the Mayflower, by Lerone Bennett, Jr., pp. 108-125.
Capitalism and Slavery, by Eric Williams, pp. 48-69.

Suggested References

Black Protest, by Joanne Grant, pp. 17-30.
A People Uprooted 1500-1800, edited by Benjamin Quarles and Sterling Stuckey, Vol. I, pp. 85-109.

For More Extensive Study

Pioneers in Protest, by Lerone Bennett, Jr.
Prince Hall and the African Lodge, by Charles Wesley.
A History of the Negro Race in the United States, Vol. I, by George Washington Williams.

Tenth Session

1. The impact of the Haitian Revolution on the slave systems of the New World.
2. The aftermath of the Haitian Revolution.
3. Slave sailors and the news of the Haitian Revolution.

Main References

The Black Jacobins, by C. L. R. James, pp. 145-198.
Before the Mayflower, by Lerone Bennett, Jr., pp. 96-126.

Suggested References

The Negro, by W. E. B. DuBois, pp. 96-109.
Chains of Slavery 1800-1865, edited by Benjamin Quarles and Sterling Stuckey, pp. 7-33.

For More Extensive Study

Black Abolitionists, by Benjamin Quarles.
The Negro in the American Revolution, by Benjamin Quarles.
The Negro in Our History, by Carter G. Woodson and Charles H. Wesley.

Eleventh Session

1. Resistance movements in the first half of the nineteenth century: The massive slave revolts.
2. The "free" Blacks in New England and in the Abolitionist movement.

Main References

Before the Mayflower, by Lerone Bennett, Jr., pp. 127-159.
From Slavery to Freedom, by John Hope Franklin, pp. 242-250.

Suggested References

American Negro Slave Revolts, by Herbert Aptheker, pp. 162-208.
Black Protest, by Joanne Grant, pp. 31-62.
The Hurricane of Promise, by Raymond McHugh, pp. 3-21.
Blacks in America: Then and Now, by Edgar A. Tappin, pp. 9-16.

For More Extensive Study

Pioneers in Protest, by Lerone Bennett, Jr.
The Black Abolitionists, by Benjamin Quarles.
The Life and Times of Frederick Douglass, by Frederick Douglass.

Twelfth Session

1. The impact of David Walker's Appeal on the thought and action of the Abolitionist movement after 1829.
2. The David Walker era.
3. David Walker's Appeal as literature.

Main References

Pioneers in Protest, by Lerone Bennett, Jr., pp. 69-82.

Suggested References

The Continual Cry of David Walker, by Herbert Aptheker.
David Walker's Appeal, introduction by David Wiltse.
Chronicles of Negro Protest, by Bradford Chambers, pp. 65-75.
The Hurricane Promise: Free Negroes before the Civil War, by Raymond McHugh, pp. 15-47.

For More Extensive Study

Great Negroes Past and Present, by Russell Adams.
Martin Delany: Father of Black Nationalism, by Dorothy Sterling.

Thirteenth Session

1. The impact of the Black elite on the Abolitionist movement, i.e., Frederick Douglass, John Russwurm, Samuel Ringgold Wad, Samuel Cornish and Henry Highland Garnet.
2. The impact of the African Colonization Society on social thought related to Black Americans.

Main References

Pioneers in Protest, by Lerone Bennett, Jr., pp. 59-197.
The Negro in the Making of America, by Benjamin Quarles, pp. 83-108.

Suggested References

Chronicles of Negro Protest, by Bradford Chambers, pp. 76-121.
Rebellion and Protest: The Anti-Slavery Crusade, by Fern Kelly, pp. 21-32.
Chains of Slavery 1890-1865, edited by Benjamin Quarles and Sterling Stuckey, pp. 61-113.

For More Extensive Study

The Slave Community, by John W. Blassingame.
The Black Abolitionists, by Benjamin Quarles.
William Styron's Nat Turner: Ten Black Writers Respond, edited by John Henrik Clarke.
Long Memory, by Mary F. Berry and John W. Blassingame.

Four

AFRICA'S PLACE IN AFRICAN-AMERICAN HISTORY FROM THE RECONSTRUCTION TO THE PRESENT

A detailed survey of the main events in African-American history from the period of the Reconstruction to the present. The intent of the beginning of this reading guide is to show that the Civil War, the Reconstruction and its aftermath are pivotal events in American history whose reverberations still affect the political structure of America. Other major topics are:

Black America at the end of the nineteenth century
The Booker T. Washington Era
W. E. B. DuBois and the new Black Radical Elite
Black Americans in the First World War
The rise and fall of the Garvey Movement
Blacks in the Great Depression

Black Americans in the Second World War
The rise of the Civil Rights and Black Power movements after
  World War II

Because early African-American history is inseparable from African history, it is important for students in this course to have at least a basic background knowledge of what happened in Africa before the slave trade. There is also an urgent need for simple and direct information on how and why the slave trade came. For that reason, there are a number of books on the suggested reading list that deal with the African background and the relationship African history has to both African-American history and world history in general.

In particular, students should note the following books which are essential for this background. Among the reissues of *The Negro*, by W. E. B. DuBois, which are especially important, combined with Dr. Boahen's *Topics in West African History*, is a good overview of West Africa prior to and after the start of the slave trade. *African Background Outlined*, by Carter G. Woodson, gives a world view of the African people before and after this greatest of human tragedies.

First Session

1. The Civil War, Emancipation, the New Freedom and New Illusions: Black political power brief and fleeting to 1875.
2. Background to the conflict: What was the North fighting for? What was the South fighting for? Why was the issue of slavery so easily lost as a cause for this conflict?
3. Black soldiers in the Civil War: Who were they and why did they fight?

Second Session

1. President Lincoln and the Civil War: The second phase.

Main References

The Betrayal of the Negro, by Rayford Logan, pp. 11-23.
Before the Mayflower, by Lerone Bennett, Jr., pp. 160-219.

Suggested References

Negro Social and Political Thought, by Howard Brotz, pp. 226-297.
Forward to Freedom, Mr. Lincoln and the Negroes, by Grassie H. Hudson, pp. 3-37.

For More Extensive Study

Black Reconstruction, by W. E. B. DuBois.
Emancipation, by John Hope Franklin.
The Burden of Southern History, by C. Vann Woodward.

Third Session

1. Reconstruction: Black political ascending: A short day in the sun.

Fourth Session

1. Reconstruction: The last phase.

Main References

Black Power U.S.A., by Lerone Bennett, Jr..
Before the Mayflower, by Lerone Bennett, Jr., pp. 127-219.

Suggested References

The Betrayal of the Negro, by Rayford Logan, pp. 11-23.
The Lost Promise: Reconstruction in the South, by Dr. W. Sherman
  Jackson, pp. 3-19.
Black Reconstruction in America 1860-1880, by W. E. B. DuBois.

For More Extensive Study

The Burden of Southern History, by C. Vann Woodward.
Emancipation, by John Hope Franklin.
The World the Slaves Made, by Eugene Genovese.
The Slave Community, by John Blassingame.

Fifth Session

1. The betrayal of the Reconstruction and the emergence of the
   Booker T. Washington Era.

Sixth Session

1. Black politicians and their white "allies."

Main References

The Betrayal of the Negro, by Rayford Logan, pp. 165-313.
Before the Mayflower, by Lerone Bennett, Jr., pp. 228-274.

From Slavery to Freedom, by John Hope Franklin, pp. 297-323.

Suggested References

Pioneers in Protest, by Lerone Bennett, Jr., pp. 102-114.
The Lost Promise: Reconstruction in the South, by Dr. W. Sherman Jackson, pp. 7-47.
Separate and Unequal, edited by Benjamin Quarles and Sterling Stuckey, pp. 6-36.

For More Extensive Study

The Reconstruction, by W. E. B. DuBois.
There Is a River, by Vincent Harding.
A History of the Negro Race in the United States, Vols. I and II, by George Washington Williams.

Seventh Session

1. The making of Black institutions before and after the betrayal of the Reconstruction.

Eighth Session

1. The Booker T. Washington Era.

Main References

Pioneers in Protest, by Lerone Bennett, Jr., pp. 274-322.
From Slavery to Freedom, by John Hope Franklin, pp. 389-449.

Suggested References

The Negro Vanguard, by Richard Bardolph, pp. 55-195.
Negro Makers of History, by Carter G. Woodson and Charles Wesley, pp. 260-335.

Booker T. Washington and His Critics, published by Heath.
Up from Slavery, by Booker T. Washington.
The Reign of Jim Crow: Separatism and the Black Response, by Dr. Robert E. Moran.
The Souls of Black Folk, by W. E. B. DuBois.
Black Titan: W. E. B. DuBois, by John Henrik Clarke, Beacon Press, 1970.

For More Extensive Study

Black Exodus, by Edwin S. Redkey.
Men of Mark, by William J. Simmons.
The Life and Times of Booker T. Washington, by Louis Hollins.

Ninth Session

1. Black America enters the twentieth century: new dreams and new illusions.

Main References

From Slavery to Freedom, by John Hope Franklin, pp. 382-433.
American Negro, Old World Background, New World Experience, by Logan and Cohen, Chapter 7, pp. 153-182.

Suggested References

Black Exodus, by Edwin S. Redkey, pp. 1-46.
Northward Bound: From Sharecropping to City Living, by Dr. Oscar E. Williams, pp. 3-18.

For More Extensive Study

Out of the House of Bondage, by Kelley Miller.
The Souls of Black Folk, by W. E. B. DuBois.
The Gift of Black Folk, by W. E. B. DuBois.
The Burden of Southern History, by C. Vann Woodward.

The Strange Career of Jim Crow, by C. Vann Woodward.
The Rise and Fall of "Jim Crow," 1865-1964, by Frank B. Latham.

Tenth Session

1. W. E. B. DuBois and the new Black leadership: A challenge to the Booker T. Washington Era.

Eleventh Session

1. Pan-African nationalism and survival.

Main References

Black Exodus, by Edwin S. Redkey, pp. 252-310.
From Slavery to Freedom, by John Hope Franklin, pp. 546-576.

Suggested References

Black Protest, by Joanne Grant, latter part of the book.
From Slavery to Freedom, by John Hope Franklin, pp. 433-452.
Before the Mayflower, by Lerone Bennett, Jr., pp. 274-327.

For More Extensive Study

Pan-Africanism or Communism, by George Padmore.
Pan-Africanism: A Brief History of an Idea in the African World, by John Henrik Clarke.
Long Memory: The Black Experience in America, by Mary Frances Berry and John Blassingame.

Twelfth Session

1. Black America in the First World War.

Thirteenth Session

1. Black Exodus 1915-1920.

Main References

From Slavery to Freedom, by John Hope Franklin, pp. 333-353.
Black America, by Eric Foner, pp. 324-348.

For More Extensive Study

Anyplace But Here, by Arna Bontemps.
Black Migration: Movement North 1900-1920, by Florette Henri.

Fourteenth Session

1. Marcus Garvey and Black Nationalism.

Main References

From Slavery to Freedom, by John Hope Franklin, pp. 354-371.
Black America, by Eric Foner, pp. 349-370.

For More Extensive Study

Marcus Garvey and the Vision of Africa, by John Henrik Clarke.
The Garvey Papers, Vols. 1-5, edited by Robert Hill.
Garvey and Garveyism, edited by Amy Jacques Garvey.
Pan-Africanism or Communism, by George Padmore.

Fifteenth Session

1. The Harlem Renaissance.

Main References

From Slavery to Freedom, by John Hope Franklin, pp. 372-393.
Black America, by Eric Foner, pp. 371-387.

For More Extensive Study

The New Negro, by Alain Locke.
Voices from the Harlem Renaissance, by Nathan Irvin Huggins.
The Harlem Renaissance Remembered, by Arna Bontemps.

Sixteenth Session

1. Blacks and the New Deal.

Main References

From Slavery to Freedom, by John Hope Franklin, pp. 394-413.
Black America, by Eric Foner, pp. 388-413.

For More Extensive Study

Negroes and the Great Depression, by Raymond Wolters.
The Bonus March, by Roger Daniels.
Hard Times, by Studs Terkel.

Seventeenth Session

1. The modern civil rights era.

Main References

From Slavery to Freedom, by John Hope Franklin, pp. 394-413.
Black America, by Eric Foner, pp. 414-488.

For More Extensive Study

Black Protest, by Joanne Grant.
Stride Toward Freedom, by Martin Luther King, Jr.
Martin Luther King, Jr., by William Robert Miller.

Eighteenth Session

1. Black Power.

Main References

From Slavery to Freedom, by John Hope Franklin, pp. 476-512.
Black America, by Eric Foner, pp. 482-556.

For More Extensive Study

The Negro Mood, by Lerone Bennett, Jr.
Pioneers in Protest, by Lerone Bennett, Jr..
Black Power, by Stokely Carmichael and Charles Hamilton.

Nineteenth Session

1. State of the Black nation: The present and prospects for the future. Class discussion.

Twentieth Session

1. Black History: An aspect of Black liberation.

Twenty-First Session

1. New directions in the study of Black history, Part I: The works of Lerone Bennett, Jr.

Twenty-Second Session

1. New directions in the study of Black history, Part II: Main focus, *The Shaping of Black America*, by Lerone Bennett, Jr.

Twenty-Third Session

1. Pan-Africanism reconsidered.

Twenty-Fourth Session

1. Black Americans and the Sixth Pan-African Congress.

Twenty-Fifth Session

1. The crisis of Black leadership in America.

Twenty-Sixth Session

1. The crisis in Africa and in the Caribbean.

Twenty-Seventh Session

1. The changing status of the Black Muslim Movement, Part I.

Twenty-Eighth Session

1. The changing status of the Black Muslim Movement, Part II.

Twenty-Ninth Session

1. A world view of the status of African people.

Thirtieth Session

1. Summary Session. Questions and Review.

BIBLIOGRAPHY

For this bibliography, I have selected what, in my opinion, are some of the best new books on African and African American history. I have purposely selected books that are easy to read and easy to obtain. Most of the books selected are in general circulation.

*An asterisk indicates that the book was written by an African or an African-American writer.

Adams, Russell L., *Great Negroes, Past and Present*, Afro-American Publishing Co., Chicago, 1966.

*Agebodeka, F., *The Rise of the Nation States: A History of the West African Peoples, 1600-1964*, Thomas Nelson and Sons, Ltd., London, 1965.

*Ajayi, J. F. A., and Crowder, Michael, editors, *History of West Africa*, Vols. I and II, Longman Group Ltd., London, 1971.

*———, and Espie, Ian, editors, *A Thousand Years of West African History*, Ibadan University Press and Nelson, Copewood and Davis Streets, Camden, NJ, 1965.

*Akintoye, S. A., *Revolution and Power Politics in Yorubaland, 1840-1893*, Ibadan History Series, Humanities Press, New York, 1971.

American Heritage, editors, *Discoverers of the New World*, American Heritage Publishing, New York, 1965.

Aptheker, Herbert, *American Negro Slave Revolts*, International Publishers, New York, 1963.

———, *And Why Not Every Man?*, International Publishers, New York, 1970.

———, editor, *One Continual Cry by David Walker: Its Setting and Meaning*, Humanities Press, New York, 1965.

———, *The Negro People in America*, International Publishers, New York, 1946.

———, *The Negro in the American Revolution*, International Publishers, New York, 1940.

———, *Toward Negro Freedom*, New Century Publishers, New York, 1956.

———, *Essays in the History of the American Negro*, New World Paperback, New York, 1964.

———, *A Documentary History of the Negro People in the United States*, Vols. I and II, Citadel Press, New York, 1962.

*Asante, Molefi Kete, and *Asante, Kariamu Welsh, editors, *African Culture, The Rhythms of Unity*, Africa World Press, Trenton, NJ, 1989.

Arkell, A. J., *A History of the Sudan to 1821*, The Athlone Press, London, 1961.

*Azikiwe, Nnandi, *Renascent Africa*, Humanities Press, New York, 1968.

Balandier, Georges, *Daily Life in the Kingdom of the Kongo, From the Sixteenth to the Eighteenth Century*, Pantheon Books, New York, 1968.

Bardolph, Richard, *The Negro Vanguard*, Rinehart, New York, 1959.

Barth, Heinrich, *Travels and Discoveries in North and in Central Africa*, F. Cass, London, 1965.

*ben-Jochannan, Yosef, *African Origins of the Major "Western Religions,"* Alkebu-lan Books, c/o Dr. Arthur Lewis, 725 St. Nicholas Ave., New York 10030, 1970.

*———, *Black Man of the Nile and His Family*, Alkebu-lan Books, c/o Dr. Arthur Lewis, 725 St. Nicholas Ave., New York 10030, 1972.

*———, *Africa: Mother of Western Civilization*, Alkebu-lan Books, c/o Dr. Arthur Lewis, 725 St. Nicholas Ave., New York 10030, 1971.

*———, with George E. Simmonds, *The Black Man's North and East Africa*, Alkebu-lan Books, c/o Dr. Arthur Lewis, 725 St. Nicholas Ave., New York 10030, 1971.

*———, *Cultural Genocide in the Black and African Studies Curriculum*, Alkebu-lan Books, c/o Dr. Arthur Lewis, 725 St. Nicholas Ave., New York 10030, 1972.

*———, *Africa: Mother of the Major Western Religions*, Alkebu-lan Books, c/o Dr. Arthur Lewis, 725 St. Nicholas Ave., New York 10030, 1970.

Benedict, Ruth, *Race: Science and Politics*, Viking Press, New York, 1964.

*Bennett, Lerone, Jr., *The Negro Mood*, Penguin Press, Baltimore, 1966.

*———, *Before the Mayflower: A History of Black America*, Johnson Publishing Co., Chicago, 1962.

*———, *Pioneers in Protest*, Penguin Books, paperback, Baltimore, 1968.

*———, *The Shaping of Black America*, Johnson Publishing Co., Chicago, 1975.

*———, *Wade in the Water: Great Moments in Black History*, Johnson Publishing Co., Chicago.

*———, *Black Power U.S.A.*, Johnson Publishing Co., Chicago.

*———, *Confrontation: Black and White*, Penguin Books, Baltimore, 1966.

Bergman, Peter M., and Bergman, Mort N., *The Chronological History of the Negro in America*, Mentor Books, New York, 1969.

*Berry, Mary Francis, and *Blassingame, John W., *Long Memory: The Black Experience in America*, Oxford University Press, New York.

Birmingham, David, *The Portuguese Conquest of Angola*, Oxford University Press, London, 1965.

———, *Trade and Conflict in Angola, The Mbundu and Their Neighbors Under the Influence of the Portuguese 1483-1790*, Clarendon Press, Oxford, 1966.

*Blassingame, John W., *The Slave Community: Plantation Life in the Ante-Bellum South*, Oxford University Press, New York.

Bleeker, Sonia, *The Ashanti of Ghana*, Dennis Dobson, London, 1966.

*Boahen, Adu with *Ajayi, J.F. Ade, and Tidy, Michael, *Topics in West African History*, Longman Group Ltd., Essex, England, 1986.

Bohannan, Paul, and Curtin, Phillip D., editors, *Africa and Africans*, The National History Press, New York, 1971.

*Bontemps, Arna, and Conroy, Jack, *Anyplace But Here*, Hill & Wang, New York, 1966.

*———, *The Harlem Renaissance Remembered*, Dodd, Mead and Co., New York, 1972.

Boxer, C. R., *Four Centuries of Portuguese Expansion, 1415-1825: A Succinct Survey*, Witwatersrand University Press, Johannesburg, 1961.

*Bracey, John H., Jr., Meier, August, and Rudwick, Elliot, editors, *Black Nationalism in America*, Bobbs-Merrill Co., Indianapolis, 1970.

*Brawley, Benjamin, *A Social History of the American Negro*, Collier Books, New York, 1969.

Breasted, James Henry, *A History of Egypt*, Bantam Matrix Books, New York, 1967.

Brian, David, *Slavery and the Period of Revolution*, Cornell University Press, Ithaca.

———, *Slavery and Western Civilization*, Cornell University Press, Ithaca.

Brooks, Lester, *Great Civilizations of Ancient Africa*, Scholastic Books, New York.

Brotz, Howard, editor, *Negro Social and Political Thought, 1850-1920*, Basic Books, Inc., New York, 1966.

Brown, Godfrey N., *An Active History of Ghana*, Vol. I "From the Earliest Times to 1844;" Vol. II "Since 1844," George Allen & Unwin Ltd., Great Britain, 1961 and 1964.

*Buah, F. K., *A New History for Schools and Colleges*, Book I and II, MacMillan and Co., New York.

*————, *West Africa and Europe*, Book I and II, MacMillan and Co., New York.

*Budu-Acquah, K., *Ghana, The Morning After*, Goodwin Press, London, 1960.

Burke, Fred, edited and annotated, *Africa: Selected Readings*, World Regional Studies, Houghton Mifflin Co., Burlington, Maine, paperback, 1965.

*Carmichael, Stokely, and *Hamilton, Charles, *Black Power: The Politics of Liberation*, Random House, New York, 1967.

*Cartey, Wilfred, and *Kilson, Martin, edited and with an introduction, *The African Reader: Colonial Africa*, Random House, Vintage Books, paperback, New York, 1970.

Cash, Wilbur Joseph, *The Mind of the South*, Knopf Publishing Co., New York, 1941.

Chambers, Bradford, *Chronicles of Negro Protest*, Parents Magazine Press, 1968.

*Chijioke, F. A., *Beginning History of Ancient Africa*, Longmans Green and Co., Ltd., London, 1966.

Chu, Daniel, and *Skinner, Elliott, *A Glorious Age in Africa, The Story of Three Great African Empires*, Africa World Press, Trenton, NJ, 1990.

Clammer, David, *The Zulu War*, St. Martin's Press, New York, 1973.

Claridge, W. W., *A History of the Gold Coast and Ashanti: From the Earliest Times to the Commencement of the Twentieth Century*, J. Murray, London, 1915.

Clark, J. Desmond, *The Prehistory of Africa*, Praeger Publishing Co., New York, 1970.

*Clarke, John Henrik, editor, *William Styron's Nat Turner: Ten Black Writers Respond*, Beacon Press, Boston, 1968.

*————, editor, *Pan-Africanism and the Liberation of Southern Africa: A Tribute to W.E.B. DuBois*, United Nations Centre Against Apartheid and the African Heritage Studies Association, New York, 1978.

*————, editor, *Marcus Garvey and the Vision of Africa*, Random House, New York, 1973.

*————, with the editors of Freedomways, *Black Titan: W.E.B. DuBois*, an anthology, Beacon Press, Boston, 1970.

*———, and Harding, Vincent, editors, *Slavery and the Slave Trade*, Holt, Rinehart and Winston, Inc., paperback, New York, 1970.

*———, *The Lives of Great African Chiefs*, Pittsburgh Courier Publishing Co., Pittsburgh, 1958.

*———, *History and Culture of Africa*, AEVAC Inc. Educational Publishers, Hempstead, New York, 1969.

*Clegg, Legrand H., *The Beginning of the African Diaspora: Black Men in Ancient and Medieval America*, Parts I and II, African Bibliographical Center, Washington, DC.

Cohen, David, *Shaka: King of the Zulus*, a biography, Doubleday and Co., New York, 1973.

Coleman, James S., *Nigeria, Background to Nationalism*, University of California Press, Berkeley, 1958.

Collins, Robert O., editor, *Problems in African History*, Prentice-Hall, Inc., Englewood Cliffs, NJ, 1968.

———, *African History: Text and Readings*, Random House, New York.

Cottrell, Leonard, *The Anvil of Civilization*, Mentor: Ancient Civilizations, New American Library, New York, 1957.

Crowder, Michael, *A Short History of Nigeria*, Praeger Publishing Co., New York, 1962.

Curtin, Phillip D., *African History*, American Historical Association, paperback pamphlet, Washington, DC, 1967.

———, *Africa South of the Sahara*, Silver Burdett Co., paperback, Morristown, NJ, 1970.

Daniels, Roger, *The Bonus March, An Episode of the Great Depression*, Greenwood Publishing Corp., Westport, CT, 1971.

Davidson, Basil, *Black Mother: The Years of Our African Slave Trade: Precolonial History, 1450-1850*, Atlantic-Little, Brown, Co., Boston, 1961.

———, *Which Way Africa? The Search for a New Society*, Penguin Books, Baltimore.

———, *Can Africa Survive?*, Atlantic-Little, Brown & Co., Boston, 1974.

———, *Report on Southern Africa*, J. Cape, London, 1952.

———, *The African Awakening*, J. Cape, London, 1955.

———, *Discovering Our African Heritage*, Ginn and Co., paperback, Boston, 1970.

———, *A History of East and Central Africa to the Late 19th Century*, Anchor Books, Doubleday and Co., New York, 1969.

———, *Africa in History*, MacMillan Co., New York, 1969.

———, *A Guide to African History*, Zenith Books, Doubleday and Co., New York, 1965.

——, *The Lost Cities of Africa*, Atlantic Monthly Press Book by Little, Brown and Co., Boston, 1959.

——, *The African Genius*.

——, with *Buah, F. K., *A History of West Africa to the 19th Century*, Anchor Books, Doubleday and Co., New York, 1966.

——, *The Story of Africa*, based on the television series "Africa," a Mitchell Beazley production, London, 1984.

*deGraft Johnson, J. C., *African Glory, The Story of Vanished Negro Civilizations*, George J. McLeod, Ltd., Toronto, 1954.

*Dike, K. Onwuka, *Trade and Politics in the Niger Delta, 1830-1885*, Clarendon Press, Oxford, England, 1956.

*Diop, Cheikh Anta, *African Origins of Civilization: Myth or Reality*, Lawrence Hill and Co., paperback, New York, 1974.

*——, *Civilization or Barbarism*, Lawrence Hill & Co., New York, 1989.

*——, *A History of Precolonial Africa* (in French), Présence Africaine, Paris, 1960.

*——, "The Origin of the Ancient Egyptians," pp. 27-57, in "The Peopling of Ancient Egypt and the Deciphering of Meroitic Script," UNESCO's *The General History of Africa Studies and Documents, 1 and 11*.

*Dobler, L., and *Brown, William A., *Great Rulers of the African Past*, Zenith Books, Doubleday and Co., New York, 1965.

*Douglass, Frederick, *Life and Times of Frederick Douglass, the Complete Autobiography*, with a new introduction by Rayford Logan, Collier Books, New York, 1962.

Drummer, Melvin, editor, *Black History*, Doubleday Anchor Books, New York.

*DuBois, W. E. B., *The Souls of Black Folk*, Crest Reprint, Fawcett Publications, 1965.

*——, *The Gifts of Black Folk*, Crest Reprint, Fawcett Publications, 1965.

*——, *Black Reconstruction in America, 1860-1880*, Harcourt, Brace and Co., New York, 1935.

*——, *The Negro*, Oxford University Press, New York, 1970.

*——, *The World and Africa, An Inquiry into the Part Which Africa Played in World History*, International Publishers, paperback, New York, 1965.

*——, *The Suppression of the African Slave Trade to the United States of America, 1638-1870*, Schocken Books, New York, 1969.

Duffy, James, *Portugal in Africa*, Penguin African Library, Baltimore, 1963.

El Mahdi, Mandour, *A Short History of the Sudan*, Oxford University Press, New York, 1965.

*Essien-Udom, E.U., *Black Nationalism: A Search for an Identity in America*, Laurel Edition, Dell Publishing Co., New York, 1964.

Fage, J. D., *Ghana, A Historical Interpretation*, University of Wisconsin Press, Madison, WI, 1966.

——, *A History of West Africa*, Cambridge University Press, London, 1969.

Fairservis, Walter A., Jr., *The Ancient Kingdoms of the Nile*, Mentor Books, published by New American Library, paperback, New York, 1962.

*Fishel, Leslie, and *Quarles, Benjamin, *The Black American*, Oxford University Press, New York.

Fisher, Allan G. B., and Fisher, Humphrey J., *Slavery and Muslim Society in Africa, The Institution in Saharan and Sudanic Africa and the Trans-Saharan Trade*, Doubleday and Co., New York, 1971.

Fitch, Bob, and Oppenheimer, Mary, *Ghana: End of an Illusion*, Monthly Review Press, Vol. 18, No. 3, July-August, 1966, New York.

Foner, Eric, editor, *America's Black Past, A Reader in Afro-American History*, Harper and Row, New York, 1970.

Foner, Phillip S., *History of Black Americans*, Greenwood Press, Westport, CT.

Foster, William Z., *The Negro People in American History*, International Publishers, New York, 1970.

*Franklin, John Hope, *From Slavery to Freedom: A History of Negro Americans*, Alfred A. Knopf, New York, 1980.

*——, *Emancipation*, Alfred A. Knopf, New York.

Freed, Rita E., *Ramses II, The Great Pharaoh and His Time*, Denver Museum of Natural History, Exhibition in the City of Denver, Memphis, TN, 1987.

Frye, J. D., and Oliver, Roland, editors, *Papers in African Prehistory*, Cambridge University Press, New York, 1970.

Gabel, Creighton, and Bennett, Norman, editors, *Reconstructing African Cultural History*, Boston University African Research Studies, No. 8, Boston, 1967.

Gailey, Harry A., Jr., *History of Africa from Earliest Times to 1800*, Holt, Rinehart and Winston, New York, 1970.

——, *History of Africa from 1900 to Present*, Holt, Rinehart and Winston, New York, 1970.

Gardiner, Alan, Sir, *Egypt of the Pharaohs*, A Galaxy Book, Oxford University Press, New York, 1966.

*Garvey, Amy Jacques, *Garvey and Garveyism*, introduction by John Henrik Clarke, Collier Books, New York, 1970.

Genovese, Eugene, *The World the Slaveholders Made*, Vintage Books, New York, 1971.

Gossett, T. F., *Race: The History of an Idea in America*, Schocken Press, New York, 1965.

*Grant, Joanne, *Black Protest: History, Documents and Analyses, 1619 to the Present*, edited with Introduction and Commentary, Fawcett Premier Books, Greenwich, CT, 1968.

Graves, Anna Melissa, *Africa, The Wonder and the Glory*, privately published, Baltimore, 1942.

——, editor, *Benvenuto Cellini Had No Prejudice Against Bronze*, Waverly Press, Baltimore, 1942.

Greene, Lorenzo J., *The Negro in Colonial New England*, Columbia University Press, New York, 1942.

*Hansberry, William Leo, "Africa's Golden Past," articles published in *Ebony* magazine:
1. "Life Could Have Begun in Kush," November 1964.
2. "Historical Facts Challenge Notion That Christianity Is Religion of West," January 1965.
3. "Archaeological Finds Refute West's Dark Continent Views," February 1965.
4. "Black Creativity Has Enriched Various Civilizations," March 1965.
5. "Queen of Sheba's True Identity Confounds Historical Research," April 1965.

*——, *African History Notebook*, Howard University Press, Washington, DC, 1981. Vol. I *Pillars in Ethiopian History*; Vol. II *Africa and Africans As Seen By Classical Writers*.

*Harding, Vincent, *There Is a River: The Black Struggle for Freedom in America*, Harcourt, Brace, Jovanovich, New York, 1981.

*Harris, Joseph E., *Africans and Their History*, Mentor Books, New American Library, paperback, New York, 1969.

*——, *The African Presence in Asia*, Northwestern University Press, Evanston, IL, 1971.

*Hayford, E. Casely, *Gold Coast Native Institutions*, Sweet and Maxwell, London, 1903.

Henri, Florette, *Black Migration: Movement North, 1900-1920*, Anchor Press, Doubleday, New York, 1975.

*Henries, A. Doris Banks, *Africa: Our History*, Collier-Macmillan International, Toronto, 1969.

Herodotus, *The History of Herodotus*, translated by George Rawlinson, Tudor Publishing Co., New York, 1939.

Herskovitz, Melville J., *The Myth of the Negro Past*, Beacon Press, Boston, 1958.

*Hill, Robert A., editor, *The Marcus Garvey and the Universal Negro Improvement Association Papers*, University of California Press, Berkeley, 1983. (A proposed ten volume work).

*Hodges, Norman, E. W., *Breaking the Chains of Bondage*, Simon & Schuster, paperback, New York, 1972.

Hoffman, Eleanor, *Realm of the Evening Star, Morocco and the Land of the Moors*, Chilton Books, New York, 1965.

*Hollins, Louis, *The Life and Times of Booker T. Washington*, University of Illinois Press, Chicago.

Hooker, James R., *Black Revolutionary*, Praeger Publishers, New York, 1970.

*Houston, Drusilla Dunjee, *Wonderful Ethiopians of the Ancient Cushite Empire*, Black Classic Press, Baltimore, 1985.

*Huggins, Nathan I., *Kilson, Martin, and Fox, Daniel M., editors, *Key Issues in the Afro-American Experience*, Vol. I and II, Harcourt, Brace and Jovanovich, New York, 1971.

*——, *Voices from the Harlem Renaissance*, Oxford University Press, New York, 1976.

Jackson, Henry C., *The Fighting Sudanese*, Macmillan Publishing Co., London, 1954.

*Jackson, John G., *Ethiopia and the Origin of Civilization*, Black Classic Press, Baltimore, 1939.

*——, *Introduction to African Civilizations*, Citadel Press, Secaucus, NJ, 1970.

*——, *Man, God and Civilization*, University Books, New Hyde Park, 1970.

*——, *Christianity Before Christ*, The Blyden Society, New York, 1938.

*James, C. L. R., *The Black Jacobins*, Vintage Books, New York, 1963.

Jenkinson, Thomas B., *Amazulu: The Zulus, Their Past History, Manners, Customs, and Language, with Observations on the Country and its Productions, Climate, Etc., The Zulu War, and Zululand Since the War*, Negro Universities Press, New York, 1969.

Jordan, Winthrop D., *White Over Black*, Pelican Press, New York, 1968.

Josephy, Alvin M., Jr., editor, *The Horizon History of Africa*, American Heritage Publishing Co., New York, 1970.

July, Robert W., *A History of the African People*, Scribner's Sons Publishers, paperback, New York, 1970.

*Karenga, Maulana, *Introduction to Black Studies*, Kawaida Publications, Inglewood, CA.

Katz, William Loren, *Minorities in American History*, Vol. I, "Early America, 1492-1812," Franklin Watts, New York, 1974.

*King, Martin Luther, Jr., *Stride Toward Freedom, The Montgomery Story*, Ballantine Books, New York, 1958.

Kritzeck, James, and Lewis, William H., editors, *Islam in Africa*, Van Nostrand-Reinhold Co., New York, 1969.

Kuhn, Alvin Boyd, *Shadow of the Third Century, A Reevaluation of Christianity*, Academy Press, Elizabeth, NJ, 1949.

———, *Who Is This King of Glory?*, Academy Press, Elizabeth, NJ, 1944.

*Kunene, Mazisi, *Emperor Shaka The Great Zulu Epic*, Heinemann and Co., London, 1979.

*Kveretwie, K. O. Bonso, *Asanti Heroes*, Oxford University Press, New York, 1964.

Lane-Poole, Stanley, *Story of the Moors in Spain*, Black Classic Press, Baltimore, 1990.

Latham, Frank B., *The Rise and Fall of "Jim Crow" 1865-1964*, F. Watts, New York, 1969.

*Lawrence, Harold G., *African Explorers of the New World*, pamphlet, NAACP Publications, New York.

Leakey, L. S. B., *The Progress and Evolution of Man in Africa*, Oxford University Press, New York, 1969.

Lemarchand, Rene, *Political Awakening in the Belgian Congo*, University of California Press, Berkeley, 1964.

Levtzion, Nehemia, *Ancient Ghana and Mali*, Methuen & Co., Ltd., London, 1973.

Lewis, Erwin, and Bain, Mildred, editors, *From Freedom to Freedom: Black Roots in American Soil*, Random House, paperback, New York.

*Locke, Alain, *The New Negro*, Arno Press, New York, 1968.

*Logan, Rayford Whittingham, *The Betrayal of the Negro: From Rutherford B. Hayes to Woodrow Wilson*, Collier Books, New York, 1965.

Lugard, Flora Shaw, *A Tropical Dependency*, J. Nisbet & Co., London, 1905.

McNeill, William H., *A World History*, Oxford University Pres, New York, 1967.

Maquet, Jacques, *Civilizations of Black Africa*, Oxford University Press, New York, 1972.

Massey, Gerald, *Ancient Egypt, The Light of the World*, Vols. I and II, Samuel Weiser, Inc., New York, 1970.

——, *The Natural Genesis*, Vols. I and II, Samuel Weiser, Inc., New York, 1974.

——, *A Book of the Beginnings*, Vols. I and III, Williams and Norgate Publishers, London, 1981.

*Mate, C. M. O., *A Visual History of Ghana*, Evans Bros., Ltd., paperback, London, 1964.

*Mazrui, Ali A., *The Africans, A Triple Heritage*, Little, Brown and Co., Boston, 1986.

*——, *Protest and Power in Black Africa*, Oxford University Press, New York, 1970.

Meier, August, and Rudwick, Elliott, *From Plantation to Ghetto*, Hill and Wang, New York, 1970.

*Meredith, Martin, *The First Dance of Freedom, Black America in the Post-War Era*, Harper & Row Publishers, New York, 1984.

Montagu, Ashley, editor, *The Concept of Race*, Free Press of Glencoe, New York, 1964.

Miller, Kelly, *Out of the House of Bondage*, Neale Publishing Co., New York, 1914.

Miller, William Robert, *Martin Luther King, Jr., His Life, Martyrdom and Meaning for the World*, Weybright and Talley, New York, 1968.

*Moore, Richard B., *The Name Negro - Its Origin and Evil Use*, Afro-American Publishers, New York, 1960.

Morel, E. D., *The Black Man's Burden*, Funk and Wagnalls, New York, 1905.

——, *King Leopold's Role in Africa*, Funk and Wagnalls, New York, 1905.

——, *Red Rubber*, Negro Universities Press, New York, 1969.

Morris, Donald R., *The Washing of the Spears*, Doubleday, New York.

*Motley, Mary Penick, *Africa: Its Empires, Nations and People*, Wayne State University Press, paperback, Detroit, 1969.

Murphy, E. Jefferson, *History of African Civilization, The People, Nations, Kingdoms and Empires of Africa from Pre-History to the Present*, Thomas Y. Cowell Co., New York.

*Nkrumah, Kwame, *Africa Must Unite*.

*——, *Ghana: The Autobiography of Kwame Nkrumah*.

*——, *Dark Days in Ghana*, Panaf Publications, Ltd., London, 1968.

Nordholt, J. W. Schulte, *The People That Walk in Darkness: A History of Black People in America*, Ballantine Books, New York, 1970.

*Ogat, B. A., and Kiernan, J. A., editors, *Zambia: A Survey of East African History*, Longmans, London, distributed in the U.S. by Humanities Press, New York, 1968.

Oliver, Roland, and *Atmore, Anthony, *Africa Since 1800*, Cambridge University Press, paperback, New York, 1967.

——, editor, *The Dawn of African History*, Oxford University Press, paperback, New York.

——, editor, *The Cambridge History of East Africa*, Cambridge University Press, New York.

Omer-Cooper, J. D., *The Zulu Aftermath*, Longmans Green & Co., London, 1966.

*Osei, G. K., *The African: His Antecedents, His Genius and His Destiny*, University Books, Syracuse, New York.

Osofsky, Gilbert, *The Burden of Race*, Harper Torch Books, New York, 1968.

*Padmore, George, *Pan-Africanism or Communism*, Doubleday Anchor Books, New York.

Patterson, Orlando, *Slavery and Social Death*, Oxford University Press, New York.

——, *Sociology of Slavery*, Oxford University Press, New York.

Pasha, Rudolf C. Slatin, *Fire and Sword in the Sudan*, Edward Arnold, New York, 1986.

Pollack, George F., *Civilizations of Africa: Historic Kingdoms, Empires and Cultures*, AEP Unit Books, American Education Publications, paperback, Middletown, CT, 1970.

*Quarles, Benjamin, *The Negro and the Making of America*, Collier Books, paperback, New York, 1969.

*——, editor, *Frederick Douglass: Great Lives Observed*, Prentice-Hall, Inc., Englewood Cliffs, NJ.

*——, *Black Abolitionists*, Oxford University Press, New York.

*——, *The Negro in the American Revolution*, published for the Institute of Early American History and Culture, Williamsburg, VA, by the University of North Carolina Press, 1961.

*——, and *Stuckey, Sterling, editors, *Encyclopedia Britannica Afro-American History Series*, paperback, Chicago. Vol. I *A People Uprooted, 1500-1800*, 1969; Vol. II *Chains of Slavery, 1800-1965*, 1969; Vol. III *Separate and Unequal, 1865-1910*, 1969; Vol. IV *Quest for Equality, 1910 to Present*, 1971.

Ranger, T. O., editor, *Aspects of Central African History*, Third World Histories, Heinemann Educational Books, Ltd., London, 1968.

Redkey, Edwin S., *Black Exodus: Black Nationalist and Back to Africa Movements, 1890-1910*, Yale University Press, Boston, MA, 1969.

Reindorf, Carl S., *A History of the Gold Coast and Asante*, privately published, Ghana.

*Rich, Evelyn Jones, and Wallerstein, Immanuel, editors, *Africa: Tradition and Change*, with Teacher's Manual, Random House, New York, 1972.

Roberts, Brian, *The Zulu Kings*, Charles Scribner's Sons, New York, 1974.

*Robins, Charlene Hill, *They Showed the Way*, Thomas Crowell, 1964.

*Rodney, Walter, *How Europe Underdeveloped Africa*, Howard University Press, Washington, DC, 1974.

*Rogers, J. A., *World's Great Men of Color*, Vols. I and II, edited by John Henrik Clarke, Collier-MacMillan, paperback, New York, 1972.

*———, *Sex and Race*, privately published by Rogers Publishing Co., c/o Mrs. J. A. Rogers, St. Petersburg, FL.

Rosenthal, Ricky, *The Splendor That Was Africa*, Oceana Publications, Inc., Dobbs Ferry, New York, 1967.

Rotberg, Robert I., and *Mazrui, Ali, editors, *Protest and Power in Black Africa*, Oxford University Press, New York.

Roucek, Joseph S., *The Negro Impact on Western Civilization*, Philosophical Library, New York, 1970.

Roux, Robert, *Time Longer Than Rope*, University of Wisconsin Press, paperback.

*Samkange, Stanlake, *African Saga: A Brief Introduction to African History*, Abingdon Press, Nashville, TN.

Sandford, Eva, *The Mediterranean World in Ancient Times*, Ronald Press Co., New York, 1938.

*Sarbah, John Mansah, *Fanti Customary Lore*, F. Cass, Ltd., London.

Schwartz, Barry N., and Disch, Robert, *White Racism*, Dell Publishing Co., New York, 1970.

Segal, Ronald, *The Race War*, Viking Press, New York, 1967.

Shinnie, Margaret, *Ancient African Kingdoms*, St. Martin's Press, New York, 1965.

Silverberg, Robert, *Empires in the Dust, Ancient Civilizations Brought to Light*, Chilton Books, Philadelphia, PA, 1963.

———, *Akhnaten, The Rebel Pharaoh*, Chilton Books, Philadelphia, PA, 1964.

*Simmons, William J., *Men of Mark, Eminent, Progressive and Rising*, Johnson Publishing Co., Chicago, 1970.

Slade, Ruth, *King Leopold's Congo*, Oxford University Press, New York, 1962.

Smith, Adam, *Nubia: Corridor to Africa*, Princeton University Press, Princeton, NJ.

Snyder, Louis L., *The Idea of Racialism*, Van-Nostrand, New York, 1962.

*Snowden, Frank M., Jr., *Blacks in Antiquity: Ethiopians in the Greco-Roman Experience*, The Belnap Press, Harvard University, Cambridge, MA, 1970.

Sordo, Enrique, *Moorish Spain, Cordoba, Seville, Granada*, Crown Publishers, New York, 1963.

*Sterling, Dorothy, *Tear Down the Walls*, New American Library, New York, 1970.

Tannenbaum, Frank, *Slave and Citizen, The Negro in the Americas*, Vintage Books, New York, 1946.

Tappin, Edgar A., *Blacks in America: Then and Now*, Christian Science Monitor, paperback, Boston, 1969.

Tarikh, Vol. I, No. 3, Humanities Press, New York, 1966.

Terkel, Studs, *Hard Times, An Oral History of the Great Depression*, Pantheon Books, New York, 1970.

Thompson, Vincent Bakpetu, *Africa and Unity: The Evolution of Pan-Africanism*, Longmans Green and Co., Ltd., London, 1969.

*Thorpe, Dr. Earl E., editor, *The Black Experience in America*, a series of ten pamphlets on Afro-American History, American Education Publishers, Columbus, OH, 1972.

*Van Sertima, Dr. Ivan, *They Came Before Columbus*, Random House, New York, 1976.

*———, editor, *The Journal of African Civilization*, Rutgers University, NJ. See special issues:
    Africans in Early Asia.
    Africans in Early Europe.

Vansina, Jan, *Kingdoms of the Savanna*, University of Wisconsin Press, Madison, WI, 1966.

Vincent, Theodore G., *Black Power and the Garvey Movement*, Ramparts Press, Berkeley, CA.

Von Wuthenau, *The Art of Terracotta Pottery in Pre-Columbian Central and South America*, Crown Publishers, New York, 1965.

Wiltse, David, introduction, *David Walker's Appeal*, Hill and Wang, New York, 1965.

*Washington, Booker T., *Up from Slavery*, Dell Publishing Co., New York.

Weatherwax, John M., *Picture History of Africa*, pamphlet.

———, *The Man Who Stole a Continent*, pamphlet.

*Webster, J. B., *Boahen, A.A., and *Idowuy, H.O., *The Growth of African Civilization: The Revolutionary Years: West Africa Since 1800*, Longmans Green and Co., Ltd., London.

Welch, Galbraith, *North African Prelude, The First Seven Thousand Years,* William Morrow and Co., New York, 1949.

Weiner, Leo, *Africa in the Discovery of America,* Innes and Sons, Philadelphia, 1922.

*Wesley, Charles H. *Prince Hall: Life and Legacy,* The United Supreme Council Southern Jurisdiction, Prince Hall Affiliation, Wash. D.C. and the Afro-American Historical and Cultural Museum, Philadelphia, 1977.

*Williams, Chancellor, *The Destruction of Black Civilization: Great Issues of a Race from 4500 B.C. to 2000 A.D.,* Third World Press, Chicago, 1974.

*Williams, Bruce, *The Lost Pharaohs of Nubia,* Archaeology Magazine.

*Williams, Eric, *Capitalism and Slavery,* Capricorn Books, paperback, New York, 1966.

*————, *From Columbus to Castro: The History of the Caribbean, 1492-1969,* Harper & Row, New York, 1970.

*————, *Documents in West Indian History,* PNM Publishing Co., Port of Spain, Trinidad, 1963.

*Williams, George Washington, *A History of the Negro Race in the United States,* Vol. I, Bergman Publishers, New York, 1968.

Wills, A. J., *An Introduction to the History of Central Africa,* Oxford University Press, New York, 1967.

Wilson, John A., *The Culture of Ancient Egypt,* Phoenix Books, University of Chicago Press, 1951.

Wingfield, R. J., *The Story of Old Ghana, Melle and Songhai,* Cambridge University Press, New York, 1957.

Wolters, Raymond, *Negroes and the Great Depression, The Problem of Economic Recovery,* Greenwood Publishing Co., Westport, CT, 1970.

*Woodson, Carter G., and *Wesley, Charles H., *The Negro in Our History,* Associated Publishers, Inc., Washington, DC, 1962.

*———— and ————, *The Story of the Negro Retold,* Associated Publishers, Inc., Washington, DC, 1959.

*———— and ————, *Negro Makers of History,* Associated Publishers, Inc., Washington, DC, 1958.

*————, *African Background Outlined,* Afro-American Studies Series, New American Library, paperback, New York, 1969.

*————, *African Heroes and Heroines,* Associated Publishers, Inc., Washington, DC, 1969.

Woodward, C. Vann, *The Burden of Southern History,* Louisiana State University Press, Baton Rouge, 1968.

————, *The Strange Career of "Jim Crow,"* Oxford University Press, New York, 1966.

In the study of African history there is a need to also have some knowledge of world history, especially the history of Europe. The following books are recommended for orientation on this broader aspect of history.

McNeill, William H., *A World History*, Oxford University Press, New York, 1967.

Palmer, R. R., and Colton, Joel, *A History of the Modern World*, third edition, Alfred A. Knopf, New York, 1968.

Wells, H. G., *The Outline of History*, Doubleday Publishing Co., New York, 1949.